hamlyn cookery club

Easy cake

decorating

hamlyn cookery club

Easy cake
decorating

First published in 2000 by Hamlyn
an imprint of Octopus Publishing Group Ltd
2–4 Heron Quays
London E14 4JP

British Library Cataloguing-in-Publication Data
A catalogue record for this book is available from the
British Library.

ISBN 0 600 60073 4

Printed in China

Copy Editor: Heather Thomas
Creative Director: Keith Martin
Design Manager: Bryan Dunn
Designer: Ginny Zeal
Jacket Photography: Sean Myers
Picture Researcher: Rosie Garai
Production Controller: Lisa Moore

Notes

1 Both metric and imperial measurements have been given in
all recipes. Use one set of measurements only and not a
mixture of both.

2 Standard level spoon measurements are used in all recipes.
1 tablespoon = one 15 ml spoon
1 teaspoon = one 5 ml spoon

3 Eggs should be medium unless otherwise stated. The
Department of Health advises that eggs should not be
consumed raw. This book may contain dishes made with
raw or lightly cooked eggs. It is prudent for more
vulnerable people such as pregnant or nursing mothers,
the elderly, babies and young children to avoid these
dishes. Once prepared, these dishes should be refrigerated
and eaten promptly.

4 Milk should be full fat unless otherwise stated.

5 Ovens should be preheated to the specified temperature
– if using a fan-assisted oven, follow the manufacturer's
instructions for adjusting the time and temperature.

Contents

Introduction

A beautifully decorated cake is always impressive, and making and decorating it yourself at home not only adds a unique personal touch but will also bring you great satisfaction. This book tells you all you need to know to create eye-catching gâteaux, novelty and celebration cakes.

SUCCESSFUL BAKING TIPS

For the best results, follow these simple guidelines when making cakes:
• Make sure all the ingredients are at room temperature before starting.
• Preheat the oven to the correct temperature before putting in the cake.
• If you are using a fan oven, adjust the temperature according to the manufacturer's instruction handbook.
• Use either metric or imperial measures – never both – within one recipe.
• Prepare the baking tin as directed before starting to make the cake.
• Add a little sieved flour with each egg to prevent the mixture curdling.

TESTING CAKES

When a cake is cooked, it should be well risen and starting to shrink away from the sides of the tin. If it is a sponge, it will look golden. When pressed lightly, it should spring back. Insert a fine metal skewer or the thin blade of a knife into the centre. If it comes out clean, the cake is cooked. Otherwise, replace it in the oven and bake for a further 5 minutes before retesting.

STORING CAKES

After cooling thoroughly on a wire rack, cakes can be stored in sealed containers or tins. Light sponges will keep well for a couple of days, whereas rich fruit cakes can be wrapped in greaseproof paper or foil and stored successfully for several weeks. If cream or fresh fruit are added to a cake, then it should be kept in the refrigerator.

EQUIPMENT

You will need to invest in some basic items of equipment for icing and decorating cakes. As your skills increase, you can add to your collection.
• **Brushes:** Keep a selection of artists' fine brushes handy for making icing run-outs and painting flowers and decorations.

- **Cake boards:** Covered in silver or gold foil, these come in various sizes and may be thick for fruit cakes, or thin for lighter sponge cakes.
- **Cutters:** A set of plain, round and novelty cutters is always useful. Specialist small cutters are also available.
- **Glazing brushes:** Use these for glazing cakes with apricot glaze before applying marzipan, and for brushing tins with oil or melted fat.
- **Palette knives:** These multi-functional knives with flexible blades can be used for loosening cakes from tins and spreading and smoothing icing.
- **Piping bags:** Make your own from greaseproof paper, or use a washable nylon one for piping icing mixtures, meringue and whipped cream.
- **Piping nozzles:** These are straight-sided and usually made of metal. They fit into the end of a nylon piping bag. You will need a selection of nozzles, including star, ribbon and writing tubes in various sizes.
- **Side scraper:** Use this for smoothing the icing on the sides of a cake.
- **Straight edge:** Made from stainless steel, this is used to obtain a smooth, flat finish when icing the top of a cake.
- **Turntable:** This is expensive but it makes decorating cakes much easier.
- **Tweezers:** A pair with rounded ends can be used for delicate work.

SIMPLE DECORATIONS FOR CAKES

If you're in a hurry and don't have much time to spend on the finishing touches, you may wish to consider one of the following simple alternatives:
- **Icing sugar:** Dredge the top of a sponge cake with sifted icing sugar or, for a more sophisticated finish, place a patterned doyley on top and then dust with icing sugar. Carefully remove the doyley to reveal the pattern.
- **Glacé and crystallized fruits:** For a colourful finish, cut angelica into diamond shapes or use different-coloured glacé cherries, cut into slices, halves or wedges, or arranged in flower petal shapes. Crystallized fruits make an attractive topping for a plain fruit cake, especially at Christmas.
- **Nuts:** Whole nuts, left plain or dipped in honey, caramel or sugar syrup, can be used to decorate the top of a cake. Chopped hazelnuts or walnuts, or flaked almonds, are perfect for coating the sides of cakes and gâteaux.
- **Citrus fruits:** Use the fruit and rind for decorating cakes and adding a fresh tangy flavour. Orange, lemon or lime segments or slices are perfect for decorating fresh gâteaux. Finely shredded rind can be sprinkled over a simply iced cake.
- **Flowers:** Tiny fresh flowers, sugar-frosted ones, or even silk and artificial flowers make a natural pretty decoration for cakes.

Simply Decorated

Balloon Birthday Cake

1 x 20 cm (8 inch) round Light Fruit
  Cake (see page 82)
2½ tablespoons Apricot Glaze
  (see page 77)
875 g (1¾ lb) Marzipan (see page 71)
25 cm (10 inch) round cake board
3 quantities Royal Icing (see page 71)
red, blue, yellow and green food
  colouring
2 metres (2 yards) each 5 mm
  (¼ inch), red, blue, yellow and
  green ribbon

Brush the fruit cake all over with
apricot glaze and then cover it with
the marzipan, cutting out a circle
for the top and a long strip for the
sides. Place the cake in the centre of
the cake board.

Make up 2 quantities of royal
icing and flat-ice the top and sides
of the cake with 2 or 3 coats of icing
until smooth. Leave to dry. Ice the
cake board (see page 86), reserving
the remaining icing for decoration.

Make up the remaining quantity
of royal icing and then divide into
4 equal portions. Colour one red, one
blue, one yellow and one green with
a few drops of the appropriate food
colouring. Trace the balloon and
letters for the person's name onto
the top of the cake (see page 94).

Make the balloon run-outs red, blue,
yellow and green and flood the
letters in alternative colours (see
page 87). Leave to dry.

Half-fill a greaseproof paper
piping bag, fitted with a small star
nozzle, with the reserved white
icing. Pipe a star border around the
top and bottom edges of the cake.

Fill 4 greaseproof paper piping
bags with soft-peak consistency red,
blue, yellow and green icing
respectively. Snip off the points and
pipe beads of icing in alternate
colours on top of the stars around
the top and bottom of the cake.

Carefully position the run-out
balloons and the name on top of
the cake and secure them with a
little icing. Pipe coloured strings for
each balloon with matching icing.

Measure and fit the ribbons
around the side of the cake and the
cake board. Secure with a little
icing. Tie 4 coloured bows and press
them into position diagonally
across the ribbons, with icing. Place
the cake in a box and leave to dry.

**Makes one 20 cm (8 inch)
cake**

Good Luck Cake

1 quantity 20 cm (8 inch) round
   tin Light Fruit Cake mixture
   (see page 82)
2½ tablespoons Apricot Glaze
   (see page 77)
28 cm (11 inch) round cake
   board
1 kg (2 lb) Marzipan (see page 71)
1.5 kg (3 lb) ready-to-roll icing
2 metres (2 yards) 1 cm (½ inch) wide
   green ribbon
yellow and mauve small fresh Sugar-
   Frosted Flowers (see page 90)

Grease and double-line a 25 cm
(10 inch) horseshoe-shaped tin.
Spoon the light fruit cake mixture
into the prepared tin and level the
top. Bake according to the chart on
page 83, then cool.

Brush the cake with apricot glaze
and place it in the centre of the
cake board. Cover with marzipan
(see page 86) and then leave to dry.
Cover the cake and cake board
smoothly with ready-to-roll icing.

Using a zig-zag crimping tool,
crimp the top and base of the cake.
Insert 30 x 2 cm (¾ inch) lengths of
green ribbon into the icing at 1 cm

(½ inch) intervals around the sides
of the cake and then position in the
centre. Measure and fit the rest of
the green ribbon around the board.
Just before serving, arrange the
sugar-frosted flowers on top of the
cake and inside the horseshoe.

Makes one horseshoe cake

left: balloon birthday cake
above: *good luck cake*

Heart-shaped Birthday Cake

2-egg quantity 20 cm (8 inch) round
   Quick Mix Cake (see page 80), or
   Madeira Cake (see page 81), cut
   into a heart shape or baked in a
   heart-shaped tin
6–8 tablespoons lemon curd
   (for Quick Mix Cake only)
25 cm (10 inch) round or heart-
   shaped cake board
1 quantity Apricot Glaze
   (see page 77)
pink food colouring
1½ quantities Butter Cream
   (see page 75)
silver balls
about 3–4 fresh flowers
6–7 silver leaves

If using a quick mix cake, cut it in half horizontally, spread with the lemon curd and reassemble. Stand on a round or a heart-shaped cake board. If using the Madeira cake, there is no need to fill it. Brush the cake all over with apricot glaze.

Add a few drops of pink food colouring to the butter cream to tint it pale pink and then use about three-quarters of it to completely cover the whole cake.

Stand the cake on either an icing turntable or a plate balanced on an upturned plate. Take a serrated-edged icing comb and carefully pull it around the sides of the cake, at the same time moving it up and down evenly to give a wavy line.

Next, take a serrated-edged ruler and pull it over the top of the cake, again moving it backwards and forwards to create a wavy line. The comb may be used in place of a ruler but it may need to be pulled across 2 or 3 times to cover the top of the cake totally. Alternatively, the top may be levelled with a small round-bladed palette knife in a backwards and forwards movement to give a smooth surface to the top of the cake.

Tint the rest of the butter cream a deeper shade of pink with some more food colouring. Put some into a piping bag, fitted with a plain writing nozzle (No. 2 or 3), and then write 'Happy Birthday' across the top of the cake.

Put the remaining butter cream into a piping bag, fitted with a medium star nozzle, and pipe a continuously twisted coil evenly around the top edge of the cake.

Using the same nozzle, pipe a star to attach the cake to the board but so it extends a little way up the side of the cake. Pipe a normal star next to it and continue all round the base in this way. Top each of the small stars with a silver ball.

Arrange sprays of fresh flowers on top of the cake around the writing and complete the decoration with a few silver leaves.

Makes one 20 cm (8 inch) heart-shaped cake

above heart-shaped birthday cake
right: basket of chocolates

Basket of Chocolates

2-egg quantity 20 cm (8 inch) round
  Quick Mix Cake (see page 80), or
  Madeira Cake (see page 81), cut
  into a heart shape or baked in a
  heart-shaped tin
25 cm (10 inch) round or heart-
  shaped cake board
1 quantity Apricot Glaze
  (see page 77)
brown food colouring
175 g (6 oz) Decoration Icing
  (see page 73)
1–2 tablespoons coffee essence
  (optional)
2 quantities Butter Cream
  (see page 75)
about 375 g (12 oz) assorted luxury
  chocolates
large gold bow
artificial flower

Stand the cake on the cake board
and then brush it all over with the
apricot glaze.

Add a touch of brown food
colouring to the decoration icing to
tint it to a pale coffee colour. Roll
out the icing and cut to a heart
shape, the same size as the cake.
Cut in half down the centre, place
on a sheet of nonstick baking paper
and leave to dry in a warm place.

Add brown food colouring or
coffee essence to tint the butter
cream to a pale coffee colour to
match the lid. Spread a thin layer
over the top of the cake and neaten
with a palette knife.

To work the basket weave, fit a
piping bag with a basket weave
nozzle and another with a No. 2
writing nozzle and fill both with
butter cream. Beginning at the dent
at the back of the cake and holding
the basket weave nozzle at an angle
to the cake, pipe 3 or more lines,
about 2.5 cm (1 inch) long, one
above the other and with the width
of the nozzle left between them.

Next, with the writing nozzle,
pipe a straight vertical line down
the edge of the horizontal ribbon
lines. Take the basket nozzle again
and then pipe more lines the same
length as the first ones to fill the
gaps but beginning halfway along
those already piped and covering
the straight lines. Pipe another
straight vertical line down the edge
and continue to build up the basket
weave around the sides of the cake
in this way but taking care to keep
them even.

Work the basket weave in the
same way on the dried fondant
paste heart pieces for the lid, and
pipe a squiggly line on the edge.
Leave to dry.

Arrange the chocolates round the
top edge of the cake. Build up with
more chocolates on the front half of
the cake, leaving the centre empty.

Carefully place the lids on the
cake, sticking the cut edge into the
centre and allowing the lids to rest
on the chocolates as if they are
peeping out. Place the gold ribbon
bow and the artificial flower in the
centre of the lid.

Makes one 20 cm (8 inch) heart-shaped cake

Feathered Birthday Cake

2-egg quantity 20 cm (8 inch) round
  Quick Mix Cake (see page 80), or
  Madeira Cake (see page 81)
1 or 1½ quantities Vanilla Butter
  Cream (see page 75)

25 cm (10 inch) round cake
  board
1 quantity Glacé Icing (see page 73)
green food colouring
Glacé Icing made with 50 g (2 oz)
  icing sugar (see page 73)
75 g (3 oz) coconut strands or
  desiccated coconut, toasted
25 g (1 oz) Marzipan (see page 71)
selection of marzipan fruits, made

with 250 g (8 oz) marzipan
  (see right)

If using a quick mix cake, fill it with
butter cream (use the extra half
quantity of butter cream); if using a
Madeira, leave it plain. Stand the
cake on the cake board or a plate.

Make up the larger quantity of
glacé icing and tint it a pale green

colour with a touch of green food colouring. Immediately make up the smaller amount, colour it a deep green and put it into a greaseproof paper piping bag.

Pour the pale green icing over the middle of the cake and, using a palette knife, spread it out quickly so that it almost reaches the edge (it will run to the edge by itself).

Immediately cut the tip off the icing bag and pipe straight lines across the top of the cake at 1–2 cm (½–¾ inch) intervals. Draw a skewer or the point of a knife at right angles across the lines, about 2.5 cm (1 inch) apart. Turn the cake round and quickly draw the skewer across again in between the first lines but in the opposite direction to complete the feathered effect. Leave to set.

Trim off any excess icing and then spread the sides of the cake with butter cream and coat evenly with the coconut.

Colour the marzipan a deep green with a few drops of food colouring and then roll out thinly. Cut it into a shape, approximately 6 cm (2½ inches) square with concave sides, and then position it centrally on the cake.

Put a little of the butter cream into a piping bag, which is fitted with a No. 2 or 3 writing nozzle, and pipe the words 'Happy Days' on top of the marzipan.

Put the rest of the butter cream into a piping bag, fitted with a medium star nozzle, and pipe stars around the top edge of the cake. Work a continuous twisted piped row of butter cream around the base of the cake.

Complete the decoration by adding a circle of marzipan fruits around the top of the cake. Attach them with some butter cream.

Makes one 20 cm (8 inch) round cake

MAKING MARZIPAN FRUITS:
Bananas
Roll out a little yellow marzipan into a banana shape. Paint on some stripes and markings with brown food colouring.

Pears
Form natural-coloured marzipan into a pear shape. Add a stem and calyx using a clove cut in half with the tip for the stem and the head for the calyx. Paint the pear with green and brown food colourings.

Apples
Roll natural-coloured or pale green marzipan into small balls with indentations at the top and base. Add stems and calyxes as for the pears. If using green marzipan, paint part of the apple with red food colouring. With natural-coloured marzipan, paint first with red, then blend in green colouring.

Strawberries
Mould some deep pink or red marzipan into a strawberry shape. Roll in some granulated sugar for seeds and then make a hull from some green marzipan.

Oranges and Lemons
Use orange and yellow marzipan. To achieve the texture of the skin, either prick all over with a pin head or roll on the side of a grater. Add a clove top or scrap of green marzipan for each calyx.

Grapes
Make tiny balls of pale green or mauve marzipan and stick together to form bunches.

Plums
Use deep yellowish-red or deep plum-mauve coloured marzipan. Make an indentation down one side of the fruit.

left: feathered birthday cake

Congratulations Cake

1 x 25 cm (10 inch) round Light Fruit
 Cake (see page 82)
3½ tablespoons Apricot Glaze
 (see page 77)
1.25 kg (2½ lb) Marzipan
 (see page 71)
30 cm (12 inch) round cake
 board
3½ quantities Royal Icing
 (see page 71)
blue food colouring
1 metre (1 yard) each 1 cm (½ inch)
 and 5 mm (¼ inch) fancy dark blue
 ribbons
1 metre (1 yard) 5 mm (¼ inch) dark
 blue ribbon

Brush the cake with apricot glaze and then cover it with marzipan (see page 86). Place the cake in the centre of the cake board.

Tint the royal icing pale blue with food colouring. Flat-ice the top and sides of the cake with 2 or 3 coats of blue icing until smooth (see page 28). Leave to dry. Ice the cake board smoothly. Tint two-thirds of the remaining blue icing a deeper blue with more food colouring.

Half-fill a greaseproof paper piping bag, fitted with a No. 2 plain writing nozzle, with the deeper blue icing. Pipe 60 sugar pieces, allowing for breakages, as shown in the photograph.

Make a petal template for the top of the cake. Mark the design centrally on top of the cake, using a pin. Divide the side of the cake into 6 equal sections and mark each section at the top edge with a bead of icing. Divide each section into

5 areas with beads of icing piped at the top edge.

Half-fill a greaseproof paper piping bag, fitted with a No. 2 plain writing nozzle, with pale blue royal icing. Outline the petal-shaped designs on top with a fine thread. Pipe a second line of icing following the outside of the petal shape. Pipe 3 beads of icing at the point of each scallop.

Using the No. 2 nozzle and pale blue icing, pipe a fine thread of icing on to the first bead on the side of the cake. Allow the thread to form a drop loop and join it on to the next bead. Repeat to pipe 5 drop loops. Underneath, pipe another 4 drop loops and then decrease to 3, 2 and 1 to form a side design. Repeat on the remaining 5 sections.

Pipe the word 'Congratulations' with the remaining pale blue icing across the centre of the cake, using a No. 2 nozzle. Overpipe the writing, petal shapes, beads and side loops with dark blue icing, using a No. 1 nozzle.

Measure and fit the fancy ribbons around the base of the cake and the board, securing them with a little icing. Tie 6 tiny bows with the plain ribbon and secure them to the base ribbon in between the side pattern.

Carefully remove the sugar pieces from the paper and attach them to the top edge of the cake with beads of pale blue icing. Place the cake in a box and leave to dry.

**Makes one 25 cm (10 inch)
round cake**

A Basket of Roses

1 x 18 cm (7 inch) round Rich Fruit
  Cake (see page 84)
2 tablespoons Apricot Glaze
  (see page 77)
750 g (1½ lb) Marzipan
  (see page 71)
23 cm (9 inch) round cake board
1 quantity Royal Icing
  (see page 71)
pink, red, yellow, orange and brown
  food colourings
moulded roses (see page 90)
1 metre (1 yard) pink ribbon
46 cm (18 inch) cane or wire for
  handle

Brush the cake with apricot glaze
and then cover with marzipan (see
page 86) and place on the cake
board. Colour the royal icing with a
few drops of yellow colouring and a
drop or two of brown colouring to
make the icing cane coloured. Flat
ice the top of the cake only. Cover
the side with basket work piping.
Using a large star nozzle, pipe a
shell edging around the top and
bottom edge of the basket.

 Mould some large roses, mixing
the modelling paste with food
colourings to give as many different
shades as desired. Place the roses on
top of the basket, securing each
with a little royal icing.

 Cut the ribbon in half, wind one
half around the cane or wire, secure
with a dot of icing and push the

ends of the cane or wire into the
top of the cake. Tie a bow on the
handle with the remaining ribbon.

**Makes one 18 cm (7 inch)
round cake**

left: congratulations cake
above: a basket of roses

Forever
and Always

25 cm (10 inch) round or
   horseshoe-shaped Rich Fruit Cake
   (see page 84)
875 g (1¾ lb) Marzipan (see page 71)
1 kg (2 lb) Royal Icing (see page 71)
30 cm (12 inch) round or horseshoe-
   shaped cake board
mauve and pink food colourings
5 carnations (see page 91)
6 white frilled flowers (see page 91)
a few sprigs of real green fern

To cut a horseshoe-shaped cake,
bake in a round tin of the required
size. Using a paper pattern, cut out a
central circle between 7.5 cm
(3 inches) and 10 cm (4 inches) in
diameter, depending on the size of
the cake. Place the pattern over the
cake and, using a sharp knife,
carefully cut out the centre and
then a wedge-shaped piece from the
top to make a horseshoe.

Cover the cake with marzipan
and place on the board. Colour the
icing a pale mauve.

To flat ice the cake, ice the
outside edge of the cake, then flat
ice the inside curve, using a palette
knife to sweep the icing smooth.
Allow to dry and then flat ice the
2 straight ends. Allow to dry before
flat icing the top. Repeat with a
second thin coat. Leave to dry for
24 hours.

To decorate the border, use white
royal icing and a No. 3 piping
nozzle. Pipe a row of dots around
the top and bottom edges of the
cake, on the side of the cake and on
the cake board; pipe another dot
between every second and third dot
and another dot between these 2 to
give a lace effect.

Using a No. 2 piping nozzle, pipe
the names onto the cake. Using a
No. 1 piping nozzle, overpipe the
names. Colour the remaining icing
a deep mauve and pipe tiny hearts
around the sides of the cake by
piping 2 pear-shaped dots together
as shown in the photograph.

Secure the carnations and white
flowers to the cake with a dot of
icing and then arrange a green fern
between the flowers.

Makes one 25 cm (10 inch)
horseshoe-shaped cake

above: forever and always
right: Valentine cake

Valentine Cake

23 cm (9 inch) heart-shaped Rich
Fruit Cake (see page 84)
875 g (1¾ lb) Marzipan (see page 71)
2 quantities Royal Icing (see page 71)
30 cm (12 inch) heart-shaped cake
board
pink, blue, yellow and burgundy food
colourings

Cover the cake with marzipan and
place on the cake board. Flat ice the
top and sides and allow to dry for
24 hours. If necessary, apply a
second thin coat. Allow to dry for
48 hours before applying the run-
out heart.

Using a No. 2 piping nozzle and
royal icing, pipe a smaller heart
outline on top of the cake. Soften a
little pink icing with egg white or
water until it just flows and flood
into the heart outline. Allow to dry
for 48 hours.

Using a No. 2 piping nozzle and
pink icing, pipe a scalloped outline
1 cm (½ inch) in from the edge of
the cake board. Flood in with
softened pink icing as above. Allow
to dry for 48 hours.

Using a No. 1 piping nozzle and
burgundy icing, repeat the scallop
outline on top of the run-out and
pipe pips around the edge of the
run-out. Pipe small burgundy
scallops at the base of the cake. Pipe
a matching decoration onto the
heart on top of the cake.

Using a medium star nozzle and
burgundy icing, pipe 2 rows of stars.

Outline the sides of the stars using a
No. 2 piping nozzle with pink icing.

Using a No. 1 piping nozzle, pipe
5 small dots around a centre dot for
each flower. Pipe 3 flowers – 1 pink,
1 yellow and 1 blue – and pipe the
ribbon in pink. With a No. 1 piping
nozzle and burgundy icing, make
the hearts by piping 2 pear-shaped
dots close together.

Makes one 23 cm (9 inch) heart-shaped cake

Note: If you don't have a heart-shaped
tin, use a 23 cm (9 inch) tin and cut the
cake into a heart shape. This cake can
also serve as an engagement cake. Use a
No. 1 piping nozzle with blue icing and
write the names and 'Congratulations'
on top of the heart.

Traditional Wedding Cake

When making a tiered cake it is important not to add glycerine to the first layer of icing on the top of the base cake. Therefore, when making the royal icing, do not add the glycerine until this layer is complete; then beat the glycerine into the remaining icing.

1 x 33 cm (13 inch) and 1 x 23 cm
   (9 inch) square cake boards
1.5 kg (3 lb) currants
625 g (1¼ lb) sultanas
375 g (12 oz) seedless raisins
375 g (12 oz) glacé cherries,
   quartered, washed and dried
250 g (8 oz) blanched almonds,
   chopped
300 g (10 oz) cut mixed peel
grated rind of 2 lemons
grated rind of 1 large orange
875 g (1¾ lb) plain flour
2½ teaspoons ground cinnamon
2 teaspoons ground mixed spice
½ teaspoon grated nutmeg or allspice
800 g (1 lb 10 oz) butter
800 g (1 lb 10 oz) dark brown soft
   sugar
12 large eggs
2 tablespoons black treacle
1 tablespoon gravy browning
about 150 ml (¼ pint) brandy
175 g (6 oz) apricot jam
2–3 tablespoons water
1.75 kg (3½ lb) Marzipan
   (see page 71)
5 quantities Royal Icing
   (see page 71)

To decorate:
yellow and orange food
   colouring
64 pale gold moulded roses
   (see page 91)
4 white square pillars
fresh flowers and tiny silver vase
   (see method)

Grease and line an 18 cm (7 inch) square cake tin, and also a 25 cm (10 inch) square cake tin.

Put the currants, sultanas, raisins, cherries, almonds, mixed peel and fruit rinds into a bowl and mix well. Sift the flour with the spices into a separate bowl.

Cream the butter until soft. Add the sugar, and cream again until light and fluffy and pale in colour. Beat in the eggs, one at a time, following each with 1 tablespoon of the sifted flour mixture. Fold in the remaining flour, then the treacle. Finally add all the fruit, nuts and peels and mix well.

Put about two-thirds of the cake mixture into the larger tin. Add the gravy browning to the remaining mixture and put into the smaller tin. Level the tops and then make a slight hollow in each.

Tie a treble thickness of brown paper or newspaper around the outside of the cake tins, and then place in a preheated oven, 150°C (300°F), Gas Mark 2, allowing about 2½–2¾ hours for the smaller cake and 4¾–5 hours for the larger cake, or until a skewer inserted in the centre of each of the cakes comes out clean.

Leave to cool in the tins and then turn out carefully. Prick all over the top of each cake with a skewer and pour over about half of the brandy. Wrap in foil and leave for 2 weeks. Repeat the dosing with brandy after 2 weeks and rewrap in foil and leave for 2–4 weeks or up to 3 months before proceeding.

Heat the apricot jam and water together in a pan, bring to the boil and then sieve. Brush the cakes with this apricot glaze and then cover with marzipan (see page 86). Leave to dry for 3–4 days.

Make up the royal icing, in 2 batches for ease, and pour into some airtight polythene containers. Position the cakes on the cake boards with a dab of icing. Put 2 flat coats of icing on the tops of the cakes, omitting the glycerine from the first layer on the base cake. Leave to dry between coats.

For the sides of the cakes, it is easier to ice 2 opposite sides. Leave to dry, and then ice the remaining 2 sides. This makes it simpler to get good square corners. Spread some icing on to one side of each cake, making it as even as possible, with a palette knife. Using an icing comb or palette knife, cut off the icing down the corners in a straight line and also off the top edge and around the base of the cake. Repeat with the 2 opposite sides and leave to dry.

right: traditional wedding cake

Add a second coat of icing to the sides in the same way and then give a final coat to the tops of the cakes. Leave to dry.

For the decoration, cut a square of greaseproof paper the size of the top of each tier. Fold into quarters and then draw a parenthesis bracket sign on to the paper across the corner (see photograph on page 19). Place this paper on the cake itself and prick out the same with a pin on 2 opposite corners. Turn the paper round and prick out the other 2 corners. Half-fill a piping bag, fitted with a medium writing nozzle, with white icing and pipe the outlines. Allow to dry and then overpipe.

For each corner, draw a fancy 'W' shape on paper and prick out on to the cake. Pipe outlines and, when dry, overpipe.

On the sides of the large cake, make 3 marks evenly along each side. Make 2 marks on the small cake (see photograph on page 19). When dry, overpipe. Attach 3 roses to the top of the centre loops on the large cake and 2 roses to the rest and the loops on the small cake.

Using a small star nozzle and white icing, pipe a shell pattern all along the top edges of the cakes so it falls over the edge slightly. Leave to dry. With the same nozzle and white icing, pipe alternate small stars and elongated stars round the lower edges which reach about 2 cm (¾ inch) up the sides.

Tint a little icing pale gold, using yellow and orange food colourings, and put into a piping bag, fitted with a medium writing nozzle. Pipe loops between alternate shells round the top edges. Pipe a loop or double loop from the top of the elongated star to the next, round the base of the cakes. Leave to dry.

Attach gold roses to the centre of each decorative 'W' on top of the cakes and another 1 or 2 at the lower corners of each cake.

To assemble, place the pillars evenly on the base cake and stand the smaller cake on top. Place a small flower arrangement of white freesias and/or small gold roses in a tiny silver vase on top.

Makes a two-tier 33 cm (13 inch)/23 cm (9 inch) square cake

American Wedding Cake

3 x recipe quantity lemon Genoese
  Sponge mixture (see page 80)
250 g (8 oz) ready-to-roll icing
pink and yellow food colouring
1 quantity Crème au Beurre
  (see page 75)
½ teaspoon fresh lemon juice
30 cm (12 inch) cake board
sifted icing sugar
250 g (8 oz) apricot jam
4 tablespoons water
To decorate:
about 35 silver leaves
about 55 moulded roses
  (see page 91), see method
0.5 metre (½ yard) each narrow and
  wider peach ribbons

Grease and line an 18 cm (7 inch) deep square cake tin and a 23 cm (9 inch) deep square cake tin. Spoon the cake mixture into the tins, levelling the tops and making a slight hollow in the centre. Bake according to the instructions on page 81. Remove from the oven and turn out on to a wire rack to cool. Wrap the cakes in foil or store in airtight containers for 24 hours.

Tint the ready-to-roll icing in 2 shades of peach, deeper than the crème au beurre icing will be, using pink and yellow colourings, and then knead each piece until evenly blended. Use varying amounts of peach food colouring to make about 55 roses (see page 91). Place the roses on greased greaseproof paper or nonstick baking paper and leave to dry in a warm place for 24 hours.

Colour the crème au beurre a very pale peach colour by adding 2 drops of pink colouring to the icing, and add lemon juice to taste.

Split the two cakes in half horizontally and sandwich together, using about a quarter of the crème au beurre. Keep the remaining crème au beurre covered with some clingfilm.

Place the larger cake on the cake board with the base of the cake upwards. Put the smaller cake on a thin piece of cake card which fits the cake's base, again placing the base upwards.

Heat the apricot jam with the water until dissolved and then bring to the boil. Sieve and leave to cool. Brush the glaze over both cakes and leave to stand for 30–60 minutes.

Coat both the cakes quickly with the crème au beurre and smooth as much as possible, using an icing ruler and comb and/or a palette knife dipped in some very hot water. Leave to set for 3–6 hours.

Tint the remaining crème au beurre a deeper shade of peach (to match the roses and ribbons) and place in a piping bag, fitted with a star nozzle.

Carefully position the smaller cake centrally on the larger one. Pipe a neat row of alternating shells down the corners of the two cakes and then pipe a row of shells around the top and bottom edges.

On the top corners of the cake, place 2 silver leaves and a rose, and on the other corners place 2 leaves and 3 roses. Halfway along the sides of the cakes, attach 1 leaf and 1 rose, 1 leaf and 3 roses respectively.

Attach the ribbons and the remaining roses and silver leaves with crème au beurre to make a decoration for the top of the cake.

Makes a two-tier 23 cm (9 inch)/18 cm (7 inch) square cake

Note: The completed cake will keep for 2–3 days.

below: American wedding cake

Ruby Wedding Cake

3 recipe quantities Vanilla Victoria
   Sandwich Cake mixture
   (see page 84)
1½ quantities Chocolate Butter Cream
   (see page 75)
1 quantity Chocolate Glacé Icing
   (see page 73)
75 g (3 oz) flaked almonds, toasted
33 x 23 cm (13 x 9 inch) rectangular
   cake board
about 20 red marzipan moulded roses
   (see page 91)
about 15 green marzipan leaves
   (see page 91)

Grease and line 2 rectangular tins
28 x 18 x 4 cm (11 x 7 x 1½ inches).

Make up the cake mixture and
then divide between the 2 tins.
Bake in a preheated oven, 190°C
(375°F), Gas Mark 5, for about 35
minutes until well risen, golden
brown and firm to the touch. Turn
out on to a wire rack and leave to
cool. Trim off the paper and
sandwich the cakes together with
some butter cream.

Tie a strip of double foil or
greaseproof paper round the sides of
the cake, to come about 2.5 cm
(1 inch) above the top of the cake.

Make up the chocolate glacé icing
and pour onto the cake. Spread it
out evenly and burst any air bubbles
with a pin. Leave to set, and then
remove the foil or paper.

Spread a thin layer of butter
cream around the sides of the cake
and press the toasted almonds all

over the sides. Place the cake on the
cake board.

Put some butter cream in a
piping bag, fitted with a No. 2 or 3
writing nozzle, and pipe 'Happy
Anniversary' and the numerals '40'
on the cake. Next put some butter
cream into a piping bag, fitted with
a medium star nozzle, and pipe a
top edge border of shells all around.
Pipe a border all around the base of
the cake with shells of alternating
sizes. Arrange sprays of marzipan
roses and leaves on top of the cake
and centrally at the base of the
sides, attaching them with butter
cream. Leave to set.

**Makes one 28 x 18 cm
(11 x 7 inch) cake**

Anniversary Cake

1 x 20 cm (8 inch) round tin Rich Fruit
   Cake mixture (see page 84)
2 tablespoons Apricot Glaze
   (see page 77)
25 cm (10 inch) heart-shaped cake
   board
875 g (1¾ lb) Marzipan
   (see page 71)
2 peach moulded roses
1 kg (2 lb) ready-to-roll icing
peach food colouring
1 quantity Royal Icing (see page 71)
peach pearl stamens
2.5 metres (2½ yards) each 5 mm
   (¼ inch) light peach and deep peach
   ribbons
1 metre (1 yard) fancy peach ribbon,
   1 cm (½ inch) wide

Grease and double-line a 20 cm
(8 inch) heart-shaped tin. Place the
rich fruit cake mixture in the
prepared tin and level the top. Bake
according to the instructions on
page 84. Allow to cool completely.
Brush the cake with apricot glaze
and then cover it with marzipan.

Tint the ready-to-roll icing pale
peach with a few drops of food
colouring and cover the cake and
cake board smoothly. Knead the
trimmings and cut into 3 pieces.
Colour 1 piece medium peach and
1 deep peach, using more food
colouring.

Make sprays of cut-out flowers
and 2 moulded roses (see page 91),
using the 3 shades of icing and
stamens. Half-fill a greaseproof
paper piping bag, which has been
fitted with a No. 1 plain writing
nozzle, with royal icing, and then
pipe 70 heart-shaped sugar pieces,
allowing for breakages.

Measure and fit the light peach
ribbon from the back of the cake to
slope down towards the point of the
heart at the front. Secure with a
little icing. Secure the deep peach
ribbon around the base of the cake
with a little icing. Secure the fancy
peach ribbon around the cake board
with a pin.

Carefully remove the piped sugar
pieces from the paper and attach
them to the cake just above the line
of the pale ribbon, using some
beads of icing.

Place the remaining royal icing in
a greaseproof paper piping bag,
fitted with a No. 3 plain writing
nozzle. Pipe a shell border below
the deep peach ribbon.

Tie a contrasting ribbon in loops
and bows around the sprays of cut-
out flowers and 1 of the roses. Place
on top of the cake. Put the cake in a
box and leave to dry. Attach 3 cut-
out flowers and the remaining
moulded rose to the front of the
cake board with icing.

Makes one 20 cm (8 inch) round cake

left: ruby wedding cake
above: anniversary cake

Christening Cake

1 x 20 cm (8 inch) petal-shaped Rich
    Fruit Cake (see page 84) or 23 cm
    (9 inch) round cake (see page 84)
1 quantity Apricot Glaze
    (see page 77)
750 g (1½ lb) Marzipan (see page 71)
25 cm (10 inch) petal-shaped or
    round cake board
875 g (1¾ lb) Decoration Icing
    (see page 73)
a little egg white
green, yellow, pink or blue food
    colouring
icing sugar and cornflour, for dusting
15 cm (6 inch) piece ribbon, 3mm
    (⅛ inch) wide (optional)
½ quantity Royal Icing (see page 71)
3 white or silver and white artificial
    flowers
6 silver leaves

Brush the cake with apricot glaze
and then cover with the marzipan.
If making a petal-shaped cake, press
the long side strip evenly into the
indents as you go. Cut the top
piece, using the cake tin as a guide.
Stand on the cake board and then
leave to dry.

Reserve about 75 g (3 oz) of the
decoration icing and colour the
remainder a pale shade of green,
yellow, pink or blue, kneading until
evenly blended.

left: christening cake

Brush the marzipan with egg
white. Roll out the coloured
decoration icing and use to cover
the cake, moulding it to fit over the
edges and into the indents without
leaving any air bubbles. Trim off the
edges, smooth with the fingers
dipped in icing sugar and cornflour,
and leave to dry for 24–48 hours.

Use the white decoration icing to
make a teddy bear, shaping the
pieces as in the photograph. Joint
the pieces together with dabs of
water and leave to dry. When dry, a
tiny bow of narrow ribbon the same
colour as the cake may be tied
around the neck.

To make the templates, draw a
circle of 14 cm (5½ inches) on a
piece of card, cut it out and position
carefully on top of the cake. Cut
another one 2.5 cm (1 inch) smaller
in diameter and then another
2.5 cm (1 inch) smaller than that to
give 3 graduated sizes of circles

Make up the royal icing and put
some in a piping bag, fitted with a
No. 2 writing nozzle. Carefully pipe
a line all round the outside of the
largest template. Allow to dry and
remove the card.

Put the second template inside
the piped circle of icing. Put a little
icing in a piping bag fitted with a
small star nozzle and pipe a small
circle of shells all around the
outside of the template. Allow to
dry and remove the card.

Put the smallest template in the
centre of the cake and pipe another
plain circle, using the writing nozzle.
Allow to dry and remove the card.

Using the star nozzle, pipe a
border of stars all round the base
of the cake. Next, pipe a second
star above every third star and then
a smaller one still above this. Leave
to dry.

Using the writing nozzle, work a
loop from the top of one of the stars
on the side of the cake to the next
and continue all round the base. Do
not make the loops too tight or too
loose or they will break. Pipe a small
dot directly above the joins of the
loop near the top edge of the cake
(just over the side). Work dots all
round it, then a row of loops from
dot to dot. Allow to dry.

Put another row of dots in
between the first ones and work a
second row of loops over the first
ones to give an alternate looped
pattern. Allow to dry.

Complete by working a dot on
the join of the top row of loops and
another one just above it on the
side of the cake.

Still using the writing nozzle,
pipe the name of the baby across
the circle in the middle of the cake
just below the centre. Attach the
teddy bear above it with a dab of
icing. Arrange the flowers and silver
leaves in every alternate scallop,
attaching with a dab of icing. Leave
until completely dry.

Makes one 20 cm (8 inch) petal-shaped cake or one 23 cm (9 inch) round cake

Congratulations Cake

1 x 23–25 cm (9–10 inch) round Rich
   Fruit Cake (see page 84) or Madeira
   Cake (see page 81), cut to a
   horseshoe or baked in a
   horseshoe tin
1 quantity Apricot Glaze
   (see page 77)
875 g (1¾ lb) Marzipan (see page 71)
   (for fruit cake only)
30 cm (12 inch) round cake board
1 kg (2 lb) Decoration Icing
   (see page 73)
yellow, peach and pink food colouring

little beaten egg white (for fruit cake)
icing sugar and cornflour
1 quantity Butter Cream
   (see page 75)
10–12 silver horseshoes
6–8 large peach moulded roses
   (see page 91)
5–7 medium peach moulded roses
4–5 peach rose buds (see page 90)
about 6 silver leaves

Brush the cake all over with apricot glaze and, if using a fruit cake, cover with marzipan. Stand on the cake board and leave to dry.

Colour 125 g (4 oz) of the decoration icing peach, using some yellow and pink or peach food colouring. Colour the rest a creamy colour with a little yellow and a touch of pink or peach. Roll out and use to cover the cake, brushing the marzipan first with egg white. Trim off the surplus and smooth all over with fingers dipped in icing sugar and cornflour.

Roll out the peach icing and then cut out 20 horseshoe shapes, 3 cm (1¼ inches) high. Place on nonstick baking paper, mark the nail holes with a skewer and leave to dry.

above: congratulations cake
right: traditional Christmas cake

Make up the butter cream and colour it a peach colour to match the horseshoes. Put some into a piping bag, which has been fitted with a No. 3 or 4 writing nozzle, and pipe a series of dots all around the base of the cake. Pipe a second dot above every alternate dot.

Put some butter cream into a piping bag, fitted with a No. 2 writing nozzle, and pipe a zig-zag of icing from top dot to lower dot and back again all round the base.

Using the larger writing nozzle, write 'Congratulations' in butter cream evenly around the top of the cake (see photograph).

Take the smaller writing nozzle and pipe a slanting line over the top edge of the cake all the way round, then turn the cake and pipe a second line to stretch across the edge to join up every alternate existing line to give a lattice effect. Neaten off with a dot where the lines meet.

Attach couples of horseshoes around the sides with butter cream. Make the peach roses and rosebuds, coloured to match the horseshoes. Arrange a spray of roses and silver leaves at each end of the writing, attaching them with butter cream. Leave to dry.

Makes one 23–25 cm (9–10 inch) horseshoe cake

Traditional Christmas Cake

1 x 20 cm (8 inch) round Rich Fruit
  Cake (see page 84)
25 cm (10 inch) cake board
3–4 tablespoons brandy or rum
625 g (1¼ lb) Marzipan
  (see page 71)
icing sugar, for dredging
125 g (4 oz) apricot jam
2 tablespoons water
1 quantity Royal Icing (see page 71)
red, green, blue and brown food
  colouring
10–12 marzipan holly leaves and
  berries (see page 91)

Prick the cake all over and pour the brandy over so that it seeps into the holes. Wrap in foil and store for up to 6 weeks before continuing.

To marzipan the cake, place almost half of the marzipan on a surface dredged with icing sugar, or between 2 sheets of polythene or nonstick baking paper. Roll out evenly until a little larger than the top of the cake and cut out a circle about 1 cm (½ inch) larger than the top of the cake. Set aside.

Roll out the remaining marzipan, including the trimmings, to a strip. Cut 2 lengths of string, one the circumference of the cake and the other the exact height of the cake. Using the string as a guide, cut the marzipan into 1–2 strips, the same width and circumference as the cake. Reserve the trimmings for decorations.

Gently heat the apricot jam and water in a saucepan, stirring occasionally. Sieve and allow to cool. Stand the cake on a cake board and brush the sides with apricot glaze. Fit the strips of marzipan around the cake, pressing the ends together with a round-bladed knife. Brush the top of the cake with the apricot glaze and position the circle of marzipan on top. Press the edges together with the round-bladed knife. If the marzipan is unduly moist, rub it lightly all over with some sifted icing sugar.

Store the cake, uncovered, in a warmish place for at least 24 hours, preferably 3–4 days, until dry. If the marzipan is still wet when the icing is added, the oils will seep into the icing and stain it.

To flat ice the top of the cake, put about 4–5 tablespoons of royal icing in the centre of the cake and then smooth it out with a paddling movement, using a palette knife. Draw an icing ruler or long palette knife carefully and evenly across the cake. Keep the ruler or knife at an angle of about 30 degrees. Take care not to press too heavily nor too unevenly.

Remove the surplus icing by running the palette knife around the top of the cake, holding it at right angles. If it's not sufficiently smooth, cover with a little more icing and draw the ruler across the cake again. Repeat until smooth, and then leave to dry. Add a second layer to the top of the cake in the same way, and then leave to dry.

As the sides of the cake are rough iced, add a little more sifted icing sugar to the icing so that it stands in fairly stiff peaks. Spread fairly thickly all round the sides of the cake. Using a palette knife, or spoon handle, pull the icing up into peaks all round the sides and just up and over the top edge of the cake. Leave to dry.

Tint a small amount of the marzipan trimmings red and then roll out and cut into 3 candles of differing heights. Leave to dry on some greased greaseproof paper or nonstick baking paper.

Tint and shape small pieces of yellow marzipan into flames for the candles. Leave to dry beside the candles. Attach the candles and their flames with a dab of icing.

Arrange the marzipan holly leaves and berries at the base of the candles, again attaching them with a dab of icing. Extra holly leaves and berries can be made and then stuck around the edge of the cake. Leave to dry.

Makes one 20 cm (8 inch) round cake

Round Christmas Cake

1 x 20 cm (8 inch) round Rich Fruit Cake (see page 84)
1 quantity Apricot Glaze (see page 77)
750 g (1½ lb) Marzipan (see page 71)
25 cm (10 inch) round cake board
2 quantities Royal Icing (see page 71) or 750 g (1½ lb) Decoration Icing (see page 73)
little egg white, if using decoration icing
red and green food colouring

Brush the cake with apricot glaze and use 625 g (1¼ lb) marzipan to cover the cake (see page 86). Stand on the cake board and leave to dry.

Flat ice the cake with the royal icing (see left), giving it 2 coats all over and a third on the top, and letting it dry between each coat.

Alternatively, brush the marzipan with some egg white and cover with

decoration icing or ready-to-roll fondant icing . Leave the icing to dry completely – 24 hours for royal icing and up to 48 hours for decoration icing.

Divide the remaining marzipan in half and then colour one portion red with food colouring and the other portion dark green, kneading well to give an even colouring. Use

some of the red marzipan to make 40 holly berries.

Roll out the remaining red marzipan and then cut to a 7.5 cm (3 inch) square. Place on nonstick baking paper with the holly berries and dry in a warm place.

Roll out the green marzipan thinly and cut into 20–30 holly leaves, using a special holly leaf

cutter of 2.5–4 cm (1–1½ inches) in length. Mark a vein down the centre, then put each leaf over a wooden spoon handle to curve it. Leave to dry for at least 24 hours, so that the colouring will not seep on to the top of the cake and mark it.

above: round Christmas cake

To make the template for the top of the cake, cut a circle of thick paper, about 1 cm (½ inch) smaller than the top of the cake. Fold it in half, then carefully into three, making sure each piece is exactly even. Draw a curve across the folds.

For the sides, cut a strip of paper long enough to reach right round the outside of the cake and the same depth as the cake. Fold it evenly into 6. Cut 1 cm (½ inch) off the top, then make a curved cut like that on the cake top.

Place the template on top of the cake. Put some royal icing into a piping bag, fitted with a medium star nozzle, and pipe a row of small shells to outline the template but not touching it. Leave to dry, then remove the template.

Put the side template around the side of the cake, so that it matches the top design, attaching it with a dab of icing. Pipe a similar row of small shells to outline the top edge of this template. Remove and then allow to dry.

Using a slightly larger star nozzle, put some more royal icing into a piping bag. Pipe a row of medium to large shells around the base of the cake.

Put some more icing into a piping bag, which has been fitted with a No. 2 writing nozzle (or a fine No. 1 nozzle, if preferred), and pipe a lace design between the icing shells made with the templates to fill in the shapes. This is done by moving the nozzle back and forth to give a lacy uneven pattern.

Now attach the square of red marzipan centrally to the top of the cake with a dab of icing, then, using a No. 2 writing nozzle, pipe a suitable Christmas message, such as 'Season's Greetings', on top. Decorate the cake with holly leaves and berries. Leave to dry.

Makes one 20 cm (8 inch) round cake

Square Christmas Cake

1 x 20 cm (8 inch) square Rich Fruit
   Cake (see page 84)
1 quantity Apricot Glaze
   (see page 77)
875 g (1¾ lb) Marzipan
   (see page 71)
25 cm (10 inch) square cake board
little egg white, for brushing
2 quantities Decoration Icing
   (see page 73)
icing sugar and cornflour,
   for dusting
20 green marzipan mistletoe leaves,
   20 natural marzipan mistletoe
   berries and 4 green marzipan
   holly leaves
1 quantity Royal Icing (see page 71)
1.75 metres (1¾ yards) red or green
   ribbon, 2 cm (¾ inch) wide

Brush the cake with apricot glaze and then cover with marzipan (see page 86). Stand the cake on the board and leave to dry.

Brush the marzipan lightly with egg white. Roll out the decoration icing and use to cover the cake. Mould it to fit the cake and give a rounded edge to the top of the cake (not the sharp edge achieved with royal icing). Trim off around the base and smooth all over with fingers dipped in icing sugar and cornflour. Leave to dry for about 24–48 hours.

Make the holly and mistletoe leaves and berries (see right) and leave to dry. Meanwhile, make up the royal icing.

Lay the ribbon over one corner of the cake, and then take it down to the base at the centre of the cake on the board and attach with a pin and a dab of icing. Take it up to the next corner and so on, continuing all round the cake.

Using a palette knife, add a thin layer of royal icing to the corners of the cake up to the ribbon and over the top edge corners of the cake. Pull the icing up into peaks, using the palette knife or a spoon handle. Take care not to get any icing on to the ribbon. Leave to dry. Also add rough icing to cover the cake board to the edge. The rough icing may be added before the ribbon, if liked.

Put the remaining royal icing into a piping bag, which has been fitted with a No. 2 writing nozzle, and pipe a continuous circle (or a square with rounded corners) or loops inside the ribbon on top of the cake. Leave to dry.

Attach a decoration of holly leaves and mistletoe berries and leaves to the centre of the cake with some small dabs of icing. Finally, add bunches of 3 mistletoe leaves and some berries to the cake board where the ribbon meets it, attaching them with icing, and remove the pins from the ribbon.

Makes one 20 cm (8 inch) square cake

Making marzipan mistletoe leaves and berries:
Use approximately 125 g (4 oz) natural marzipan to make leaves and berries. Take a small quantity of natural marzipan to make the berries, then colour the remainder a pale green. Roll out thinly and cut into elongated leaves with rounded edges, 2.5–4 cm (1–1½ inches) long. Mark a vein down the centre of each leaf and leave to dry. Use any scraps to make holly leaves.

Making marzipan holly leaves:
If you don't have a leaf cutter, cut the marzipan into rectangles, about 2.5–4 cm (1–1½ inches) long and 2 cm (¾ inch) wide. Using a tiny round cutter or the base of a piping nozzle, take cuts out of the edges to make the leaf shape. Mark a vein down the centre, then put each leaf over a wooden spoon handle to curve it. Set the leaves aside to dry.

above left: square Christmas cake

Gâteaux

Chocolate Hazelnut Roulade

5 eggs, separated

150 g (5 oz) caster sugar

3 tablespoons hot water

25 g (1 oz) chopped toasted
hazelnuts

175 g (6 oz) plain chocolate,
melted

icing sugar, for dusting

Filling:

150 ml (¼ pint) double cream

1 tablespoon rose water

To decorate:

14 tiny fresh rosebuds or rose petals

15 plain chocolate rose leaves
(see page 92)

Grease and line a 33 x 23 cm
(13 x 9 inch) Swiss roll tin. Whisk
the egg yolks and sugar over a
saucepan of simmering water until
thick and pale. Remove the bowl
from the heat. Add the water and
hazelnuts to the melted chocolate
and stir until well blended. Add to
the egg mixture, folding in carefully
with a spatula until evenly mixed.

Using clean beaters, stiffly whisk
the egg whites in a clean, dry bowl.
Carefully fold into the chocolate
mixture until all the egg white has
been incorporated.

Pour the cake mixture into the
prepared tin, tilting it to level the
surface. Bake in the centre of a
preheated oven, 200°C (400°F), Gas
Mark 6, for 15–20 minutes or until
the cake springs back when lightly
pressed in the centre. Leave the cake
to cool in the tin, covered with a
clean, damp tea towel.

To make the filling, whip the
cream and rose water until thick.
Place 2 tablespoons of whipped
cream in a piping bag, fitted with a
small star nozzle.

Invert the cake on to a sheet of
nonstick baking paper dusted with
icing sugar. Carefully remove the
lining paper and trim off the edges
of the cake to give a neat finish.

Spread the remaining cream evenly
over the cake. Roll it up firmly from
the far side short edge, using the
paper to help make a neat roll. Place
the roulade on a serving plate with
the join underneath.

Dust the roulade with icing sugar
and pipe a decorative rope of cream
down the centre. Keep cool until
required. Decorate the cake with
fresh rosebuds or rose petals and
some chocolate rose leaves just
before serving.

Makes one 33 cm (13 inch) roulade

below: chocolate hazelnut roulade
right: chestnut caramel gâteau

Chestnut Caramel Gâteau

1 quantity Genoese Sponge mixture
   (see page 80)

Filling:

250 g (8 oz) unsweetened chestnut
   purée

4 tablespoons freshly squeezed
   orange juice

2 teaspoons grated orange rind

1 tablespoon clear honey

150 ml (¼ pint) whipping
   cream

To decorate:

10 fresh chestnuts or brazil nuts,
   shelled and skinned

1 quantity Caramel (see page 77)

Grease and line a 20 cm (8 inch)
round cake tin. Pour the Genoese
Sponge mixture into the tin and
bake in the centre of a preheated
oven, 180°C (350°F), Gas Mark 4,
for 40–45 minutes until the cake
springs back when lightly pressed in
the centre. Turn the cake out of the
tin, remove the paper and leave the
cake to cool on a wire rack.

To make the filling, beat together
the chestnut purée, orange juice,
orange rind and honey or work in a
food processor until smooth. Whip
the cream until thick and place one-
third in a piping bag, fitted with a
small star nozzle. Fold the chestnut
filling into the remaining cream.

Split the cake horizontally into
3 thin layers, using a sharp knife.
Place the top layer on a wire rack.
Line a baking sheet with foil and
brush lightly with oil.

Dip the chestnuts carefully into
hot caramel to coat them evenly,
and then place them on a sheet of
foil, spaced well apart, to set.

Pour half of the remaining
caramel over the top layer of the
cake to cover it thinly. Pour the
remaining caramel on to the oiled
foil in a thin layer and leave to cool.
Quickly mark the top of the cake
into 10 equal wedges, using an oiled
knife. Leave to cool.

Sandwich the remaining cake
layers together, using two-thirds of
the chestnut filling. Place the
caramel layer on top. Spread the
sides of the cake evenly with the
remaining filling.

Crush the caramel on the foil
with a rolling pin until fairly fine.
Use to coat the sides of the gâteau.
Pipe a cream border around the top
and decorate with swirls of cream,
topped with caramel-coated
chestnuts or brazil nuts.

**Makes one 20 cm (8 inch)
round gâteau**

Gâteau au Chocolat

3 eggs

140 g (4½ oz) caster sugar

50 g (2 oz) plain flour

25 g (1 oz) cocoa

Chocolate caraque:

75 g (3 oz) plain chocolate

Butter cream:

2 egg whites

125 g (4 oz) icing sugar

125 g (4 oz) unsalted butter

50 g (2 oz) plain chocolate, melted

Grease and line a 23 cm (9 inch) moule-à-manque tin (see page 41). Put the eggs and sugar in a heatproof bowl and whisk over a pan of boiling water until thick. (The hot water is unnecessary if using an electric whisk.) Sift and fold in the flour and cocoa. Pour into the prepared tin and bake in a preheated oven, 190°C (375°F), Gas Mark 5, for 35–40 minutes. Turn out on to a wire rack to cool.

To make the caraque, melt the chocolate on a plate over a pan of hot water. Spread thinly on a board, leave until nearly set, then shave it off into curls with a sharp knife.

To make the butter cream, whisk the egg whites and icing sugar together over a pan of simmering water until the mixture holds its shape. Cool slightly. Cream the butter until soft, then add the meringue mixture, a little at a time. Stir in the melted chocolate.

Split the cake in half, and then sandwich together with some of the butter cream, and use the rest to cover the cake. Decorate with the chocolate caraque.

Makes one 23 cm (9 inch) gâteau

Chocolate and Chestnut Gâteau

75 g (3 oz) plain chocolate

2 tablespoons water

4 eggs, separated

250 g (8 oz) caster sugar

375 g (12 oz) chestnuts, cooked and
  pushed through a sieve

To decorate:

300 ml (½ pint) double cream,
  whipped

1 marron glacé, sliced

Line and grease two 20 cm (8 inch)
sandwich tins. Melt the chocolate
and water in a heatproof bowl over
a pan of hot water. Add the egg
yolks and sugar and whisk until
thick enough to leave a trail. Whisk
the egg whites in a clean, dry bowl
until stiff and fold into the mixture
with the chestnuts.

Turn into the prepared tins and
bake in a preheated oven, 180°C
(350°F), Gas Mark 4, for 35–40
minutes. Leave for a few minutes,
and then turn out onto a wire rack
to cool.

Use half of the whipped cream to
sandwich the cakes together. Spread
2 tablespoons cream over the top of
the cake and pipe the remainder in
rosettes to decorate. Place a piece of
marron glacé on each rosette.

**Makes one 20 cm (8 inch)
gâteau**

Gâteau Normande

3-egg quantity Whisked Sponge
  mixture (see page 79)

500 g (1 lb) apples, peeled, cored and
  sliced

2 tablespoons apricot jam

50 g (2 oz) sultanas

50 g (2 oz) raisins

2 tablespoons soft brown
  sugar

300 ml (½ pint) double cream,
  whipped

Grease and line a 23 cm (9 inch)
round tin. Prepare the sponge
mixture (see page 79), and bake in a
preheated oven, 160°C (325°F), Gas
Mark 3, for 50–55 minutes. Turn out
and cool on a wire rack.

Cook the apples and apricot jam
in a covered pan over a gentle heat
until soft. Stir in the sultanas,
raisins and sugar and set aside to
cool.

Split the cake in half and then
sandwich together with the apple
filling and one-third of the whipped
cream. Swirl another third of the
cream over the top of the cake and
pipe the remainder in rosettes
around the edge.

**Makes one 23 cm (9 inch)
gâteau**

left: gâteau au chocolat
below: gâteau Normande

Chocolate Vacherin

4 egg whites

½ teaspoon cream of tartar

250 g (8 oz) caster sugar

125 g (4 oz) chopped roasted
   hazelnuts, ground

Filling:

150 g (5 oz) plain chocolate, melted

1 tablespoon dark rum

300 ml (½ pint) whipping cream

375 g (12 oz) redcurrants

To decorate:

50 g (2 oz) chopped roasted
   hazelnuts

fresh redcurrant leaves

12 Chocolate Cut-out Pieces
   (see page 93)

Grease two 20 cm (8 inch) round sandwich tins and line with nonstick baking paper. Whisk the egg whites and cream of tartar until stiff. Gradually add the sugar, whisking well after each addition, until the meringue is thick.

Add the ground hazelnuts to the meringue and carefully fold them in, using a spatula, until evenly blended. Divide this mixture between the prepared tins and level the tops. Bake in the centre of a preheated oven, 190°C (375°F), Gas Mark 5, for 45–50 minutes until firm to the touch. Let the meringues cool in the tins before turning them out carefully and removing the backing paper.

Reserve 2 tablespoons of melted chocolate for the decoration, then stir the rum and 2 tablespoons of cream into the rest of the melted chocolate. Whip the remaining cream until thick and then place 2 tablespoons in a piping bag, fitted with a small star nozzle.

Add the rum-flavoured chocolate to the remaining whipped cream and fold it in carefully, using a spatula, until evenly blended. Sandwich the meringue layers together with two-thirds of the chocolate cream and three-quarters of the redcurrants. Spread the sides with the remaining chocolate cream and coat evenly with the chopped roasted hazelnuts.

Place half of the reserved melted chocolate in a greaseproof paper piping bag, snip off the point and drizzle a continuous thread of chocolate backwards and forwards across the top of the gateau. Dip the reserved redcurrants into the remaining melted chocolate and leave to set on greaseproof paper.

Pipe a shell border of cream around the top edge of the gâteau. Decorate with the chocolate-dipped redcurrants, redcurrant leaves and chocolate cut-out pieces and serve.

**Makes one 20 cm (8 inch)
round gâteau**

Strawberry Mallow Slice

125 g (4 oz) plain chocolate

75 g (3 oz) marshmallows

3 tablespoons dry or sweet sherry

300 ml (½ pint) double cream

3 tablespoons orange juice

2 packets sponge fingers

250 g (8 oz) strawberries, sliced

To decorate:

150 ml (¼ pint) whipping cream,
  whipped

chocolate-dipped strawberries
  (see note)

First, line the base and sides of a 1 kg (2 lb) loaf tin with nonstick baking paper. To make the filling, place the chocolate, marshmallows and 1 tablespoon of sherry in a heatproof basin set over a saucepan of hot water. Stir occasionally until the chocolate and marshmallows have melted and the mixture is smooth. Leave to cool.

Whip the double cream until it is thick. Fold half into the chocolate mixture, using a spatula, until it is evenly blended. Reserve the rest of the whipped cream.

Mix the orange juice and the remaining sherry together in a shallow dish. Dip the unsugared side of 9 sponge fingers into the juice mixture and place them, sugared-side downwards, in the base of the prepared tin. Spread the fingers with half of the chocolate mixture and cover with half of the sliced strawberries. Spread with half of the remaining cream. Repeat this layering with the sponge fingers, chocolate mixture, strawberries and cream. Finish with a layer of sponge fingers, and pour over any leftover juice. Cover and then chill in the refrigerator for several hours or overnight.

Remove the cover from the tin and invert the cake on to a serving plate. Carefully peel off the lining paper. Spread the top and sides with three-quarters of the whipping cream, smoothing it with a palette knife. Place the remaining cream in a piping bag, fitted with a small star nozzle. Pipe a cream border at the top and bottom, and decorate with chocolate-dipped strawberries.

Makes one 1 kg (2 lb) cake

Note: To make the chocolate-dipped strawberries, just melt some plain chocolate and then dip in some fresh strawberries to cover the bases only, leaving the tops and calyxes visible. Leave the chocolate-dipped strawberries to set on some nonstick baking paper.

left: chocolate vacherin
above: strawberry mallow slice

Gâteau aux Fraises

3 eggs, separated
125 g (4 oz) caster sugar
grated rind and juice of ½ lemon
50 g (2 oz) semolina
25 g (1 oz) ground almonds
To decorate:
300 ml (½ pint) double cream,
   whipped
250 g (8 oz) strawberries, halved
4 tablespoons redcurrant jelly
2 teaspoons water
50 g (2 oz) almonds, chopped and
   toasted

Grease, line and lightly flour a
23 cm (9 inch) moule-à-manque tin.
Cream the egg yolks with the sugar,
lemon rind and juice until thick.

Stir in the semolina and ground
almonds. Whisk the egg whites in a
clean, dry bowl until stiff and then
fold into the mixture.

Turn the cake mixture into the
prepared tin and then bake in a
preheated oven, 180°C (350°F), Gas
Mark 4, for 35–40 minutes. Turn out
onto a wire rack to cool.

Split the cake in half horizontally
and sandwich together with three-
quarters of the whipped cream.
Arrange the strawberries on the top.

Heat the redcurrant jelly with the
water, sieve, reheat and use to glaze
the strawberries and sides of the
cake. Press the toasted almonds
around the sides and pipe the
remaining cream around the top to
decorate.

**Makes one 23 cm (9 inch)
gâteau**

Gâteau Moka

1 x 23 cm (9 inch) Genoese Sponge
   (see page 80)
1 quantity Butter Cream
   (see page 75)
1 tablespoon coffee essence
To decorate:
125 g (4 oz) flaked almonds
icing sugar, for dusting

Split the genoese sponge in half.
Flavour the butter cream with the
coffee essence and use some of it to
sandwich the sponge together.

Spread the remaining butter
cream over the top and sides of the
cake. Decorate with the almonds.
Sift a little icing sugar over the top.

**Makes one 23 cm (9 inch)
gâteau**

Orange Gâteau Caraque

1 quantity Orange Victoria Sandwich
  Cake mixture (see page 84)
6 tablespoons orange liqueur
2 tablespoons orange juice or squash
1 quantity chocolate Crème au Beurre
  (see page 75)
about 175 g (6 oz) orange curd
about 75 g (3 oz) plain chocolate,
  grated or made into curls
  (see page 92)
Chocolate Caraque for the top
  (see page 34)
icing sugar, for dredging

Grease and line a 28 x 18 x 4 cm
(11 x 7 x 1½ inch) rectangular tin.
Spoon the cake mixture into the tin
and then bake in a preheated oven,
190°C (375°F), Gas Mark 5, for
25–30 minutes or until well risen,
golden brown and firm to the touch.
Turn out on to a wire rack and leave
until cold. Peel off the paper.

Combine the liqueur and orange
juice or squash and sprinkle all over
the cake. Leave for about 1 hour.

Make up the chocolate crème au
beurre.

Cut the cake in half lengthways
to give 2 slabs, about 28 x 9 cm
(11 x 3½ inches) each. Sandwich
together with the orange curd.

Use the crème au beurre to mask
the cake completely and then press
the grated chocolate or curls to the
sides with a palette knife. Arrange a
layer of chocolate caraque along the
top of the gâteau and leave for at
least 1 hour for the flavours to
marry. Before serving, dredge the
top lightly with sifted icing sugar.

Makes one 28 x 18 cm (11 x 7 inch) rectangular gâteau

far left: gâteau aux fraises
left: gâteau moka
above: orange gâteau caraque

Japonaise Basket

125 g (4 oz) ground almonds

50 g (2 oz) cornflour

1 teaspoon almond essence

3 egg whites

150 g (5 oz) caster sugar

25 g (1 oz) flaked almonds

Filling:

125 g (4 oz) trifle sponges

2 tablespoons Madeira or sweet
sherry

150 ml (¼ pint) whipping cream

375 g (12 oz) small mixed soft fruits,
e.g. cherries, raspberries,
redcurrants, blueberries and fraises
des bois

1 quantity Pastry Cream
(see page 76)

To decorate:

1 metre (1 yard) pink ribbon, 5mm
(¼ inch) wide

small fresh flowers and fruit leaves

Line 4 baking sheets with nonstick baking paper and then draw an 18 cm (7 inch) circle on each piece. Turn the baking paper over.

In a bowl, mix the ground almonds, cornflour and almond essence into fine crumbs. In a clean, dry bowl, whisk the egg whites until they are stiff. Gradually add the sugar, whisking until the meringue stands in peaks.

Add the almond mixture to the meringue and fold in carefully. Place three-quarters of the mixture in a piping bag, fitted with a 1 cm (½ inch) plain nozzle. Pipe a ring of the mixture inside the marked lines on each piece of paper. Continue piping in a coil to fill in the centre of one of the rings. Cook in a preheated oven, 160°C (325°F), Gas Mark 3, for 35–40 minutes until the 3 rings are firm. Remove them all from the oven and loosen each ring.

Spoon a little of the reserved mixture into the piping bag and pipe a few dots on to the edge of the base layer. Place 1 ring on top. Repeat to form a basket.

Spread the outsides with the remaining japonaise and press on the flaked almonds. Return to the oven for a further 30 minutes to set. Cool on paper on a wire rack.

Crumble the trifle sponges into a bowl and sprinkle with the Madeira. Whip the cream until thick and place 2 tablespoons in a piping bag, fitted with a star nozzle. Fold half of the mixed fruit into the remaining whipped cream.

Carefully remove the paper from the basket base and place on a plate. Spoon the sponge mixture into the basket, spread with pastry cream and top with the fruit and cream mixture. Arrange the remaining soft fruit on top. Pipe a cream border around the top edge of the basket.

Tightly fold an 18 cm (7 inch) length of foil. Wind ribbon around the foil and secure. Tie a bow to one side and place the handle over the basket. Decorate with fresh flowers and fruit leaves.

Makes one 18 cm (7 inch) basket

above: japonaise basket
right: amaretti fruit torte

Amaretti Fruit Torte

A moule-à-manque tin is a classic French cake tin with sloping sides. If you have not got one, use a 20 cm (8 inch) round cake tin instead.

3-egg quantity Whisked Sponge mixture (see page 79)
3 nectarines, pitted and very thinly sliced
250 g (8 oz) raspberries
65 g (2½ oz) packet Amaretti di Saronno biscuits
300 ml (½ pint) whipping cream
sprig of mint

Grease, base-line and lightly flour a 19 cm (7½ inch) moule-à-manque tin. Pour the sponge mixture into the prepared tin and then tilt to level the top. Bake in the centre of a preheated oven, 180°C (350°F), Gas Mark 4, for 30–35 minutes or until the cake springs back when lightly pressed in the centre.

Loosen the edge of the cake with a palette knife before turning it out of the tin. Remove the paper and leave the cake to cool on a wire rack.

Reserve 20 nectarine slices and 12 raspberries for decoration. Chop the remaining nectarines and place them in a bowl with the rest of the raspberries. Lightly crush the Amaretti biscuits. Add two-thirds to the fruit in the bowl, reserving the remainder for coating the sides of the gâteau.

Whip the cream until thick and place 2 tablespoons in a piping bag, fitted with a small star nozzle. Fold half of the remaining cream into the fruit mixture until it is evenly blended.

Cut the cake in half horizontally to give 2 layers. Spread the cream and fruit mixture on to the base layer. Replace the top layer. Spread the top and sides of the gâteau with the remaining cream and then coat the sides evenly with the remaining crushed Amaretti biscuits.

Arrange the nectarine slices in the centre of the gâteau and pipe a cream border around the top edge. Place 3 of the reserved raspberries in the centre of the gâteau with the sprig of mint and use the remaining raspberries to decorate the cream.

Makes one 19 cm (7½ inch) round gâteau

Gâteau Japonaise

375 g (12 oz) strawberries, hulled and
  sliced
1-egg quantity Quick Mix Cake
  mixture (see page 80)
Japonaise:
75 g (3 oz) ground almonds
125 g (4 oz) caster sugar
2 egg whites
To decorate:
300 ml (½ pint) double cream
3 tablespoons Kirsch
2 tablespoons crunchy nut topping
2 tablespoons strawberry jam
1 teaspoon water

Grease and line a 20 cm (8 inch)
sandwich tin. Stir 125 g (4 oz) of the
strawberries into the cake mixture,
pour into the tin and then bake for
20–25 minutes in a preheated oven,
160°C (325°F), Gas Mark 3, until
well risen and firm to the touch.
Turn out to cool on a wire rack.

Make the japonaise: mix the
ground almonds and 50 g (2 oz) of
the sugar together in a bowl. Whisk
the egg whites in a clean, dry bowl
until stiff, then whisk the remaining
sugar into them until the mixture
holds soft peaks. Add the almond
mixture and fold in well.

Line 2 baking sheets with some
nonstick baking paper and draw a
19 cm (7½ inch) circle on each.
Place the mixture in a piping bag,
fitted with a 1 cm (½ inch) plain
nozzle, and pipe over the circles.

Place one baking sheet just above
and one just below the centre of a
preheated oven, 160°C (325°F), Gas
Mark 3, and bake for 30–35 minutes
until lightly browned and firm to
the touch. After 20 minutes, remove
one layer and mark it into 12 wedges,
then return it to the oven for about
10–15 minutes.

Cool the layers on the paper. Cut
through the wedges and remove the
lining paper very carefully.

Put the cream and 1 tablespoon
of the Kirsch in a bowl and whip
until stiff. Place one-third in a
piping bag, which is fitted with a
small star nozzle.

Spread the uncut layer of
japonaise with a layer of cream,
then place the strawberry cake on
top. Spread the sides with cream

and coat evenly with crunchy nut
topping. Place on a serving plate.

Heat the jam and water together
until melted. Sieve and cool.

Spoon the remaining Kirsch over
the top of the cake and spread the
rest of the cream evenly over the
top. Pipe 10 thin lines of cream
radiating out from the centre and
pipe a shell edging around the top.

Position the japonaise wedges in
the cream on top of the gâteau and
fill in between with the remaining
strawberry slices. Brush generously
with strawberry glaze and pipe a
swirl of cream in the centre. Keep
cool until ready to serve.

Makes one 20 cm (8 inch) round gâteau

Scalloped Fruit Gâteau

200 g (7 oz) plain flour

150 g (5 oz) unsalted butter, softened
  and cut into pieces

50 g (2 oz) caster sugar

1 egg yolk

Filling:

1 egg white

50 g (2 oz) icing sugar, sieved

50 g (2 oz) flaked almonds, toasted

1 quantity Pastry Cream
  (see page 76)

1 red- and 1 green-skinned apple

1 tablespoon lemon juice

2 peaches, skinned, pitted and sliced

4 plums, halved

125 g (4 oz) strawberries, hulled

75 g (3 oz) green grapes, deseeded

150 ml (¼ pint) tropical fruit juice

1 teaspoon powdered gelatine

Grease and lightly flour a 24 cm (9½ inch) spring-form tin. Place the flour in a bowl, add the butter and rub in until the mixture resembles fine breadcrumbs. Stir in the sugar and egg yolk and mix to a soft dough. Knead on a lightly floured surface until smooth. Roll out half of the dough and use to line the base of the prepared tin.

Roll out the remaining dough into a 10 cm (4 inch) long roll and wrap in clingfilm. Chill the base and the dough roll until firm.

Thinly slice the roll and arrange the slices, overlapping, around the side of the tin. Press the slices together where they overlap and prick the base with a fork.

Line the base with greaseproof paper or foil and baking beans and then bake 'blind' in a preheated oven, 190°C (350°F), Gas Mark 5, for 30 minutes, then remove the beans and paper and cook for a further 10–15 minutes, until lightly browned and cooked at the base. Leave to cool in the tin, and then carefully remove the side of the tin and slide off the base.

Whisk the egg white and icing sugar over a saucepan of hot water until stiff. Remove the bowl from the saucepan and whisk until cool to give a stiff meringue. Spread the meringue over the outside of the case and coat with almonds.

Spread the pastry cream over the base. Quarter, core and thinly slice the apples and toss in the lemon juice. Reserve half of the apple, peach and plum slices, a few of the strawberry slices and a grape.

Combine all the other fruits and scatter them over the biscuit base. Arrange all the reserved fruits attractively on top. Mix the fruit juice with the gelatine and then heat gently until the gelatine has dissolved. Set aside to cool.

When the fruit juice is beginning to set, spoon it over the fruit in the flan case. Leave in a cool place until set before cutting and serving.

Makes one 24 cm (9½ inch) round flan

left: gâteau japonaise
above: *scalloped fruit gâteau*

43

German Torte

150 g (5 oz) self-raising flour

50 g (2 oz) ground almonds

125 g (4 oz) caster sugar

5 eggs, separated

3 tablespoons vegetable oil

4 tablespoons boiling water

Chocolate icing:

125 g (4 oz) plain chocolate

50 g (2 oz) butter

1 egg, beaten

125 g (4 oz) icing sugar

milk (see recipe)

Filling:

icing sugar, for dusting

500 g (1 lb) Marzipan (see page 71)

6 tablespoons plum jam, warmed

pink food colouring

Grease and lightly flour a 24 cm (9½ inch) spring-form tin. Put the flour, ground almonds, sugar, egg yolks, oil and water in a bowl. Mix with a wooden spoon and then beat for 1–2 minutes until smooth.

Whisk the egg whites until very stiff and fold one-third into the mixture, using a large metal spoon. Add the remaining egg white and fold in gently until the mixture is evenly blended.

Pour the cake mixture into the prepared tin and bake in the centre of a preheated oven 180°C (350°F), Gas Mark 4, for 50–60 minutes until well risen and firm to the touch. Turn out and cool on a wire rack.

To make the chocolate icing, put the chocolate and butter in a heatproof bowl over a saucepan of hot water. Stir occasionally until melted. Stir in the egg and icing sugar, then heat well until smooth and glossy. Add a little milk if the icing is too thick to pour.

To make the filling, lightly dust a board with icing sugar, roll out one-third of the marzipan thinly and trim into a 20 cm (8 inch) round, reserving the trimmings.

Cut the cake into 4 equal thin layers and place the bottom one on a serving plate. Assemble the cake in layers as follows: spread the bottom layer with 2 tablespoons of the jam. Spread the second layer with some chocolate icing and place on top of the bottom layer. Cover with the marzipan and spread with 2 tablespoons of jam. Place the third layer on top and spread with some icing. Top with the last layer.

Spread the whole cake with the remaining jam, then roll out the marzipan trimmings to a round large enough to cover the top and sides. Carefully place the marzipan over the cake and gently press into position. Trim off any surplus from around the base and reserve.

Place 1 tablespoon of the rest of the icing in a piping bag, fitted with a small star nozzle. Warm the remainder, if necessary, and then pour over the cake and spread over the top and round the sides with a palette knife. Leave for a few minutes to set.

Colour the marzipan trimmings with a few drops of pink food colouring and mould into 12 little

flowers. Pipe 12 swirls of chocolate icing on top of the cake and place a flower on each.

When cutting the cake into layers, firstly cut the cake in half, then split each half into 2 layers. The layers are intended to be very thin as the gâteau should be made up of many layers.

Makes one 24 cm (9½ inch) round cake

Scandinavian Plum Tart

The pastry case for the tart can be made in advance if time is short, and then chilled until ready to fill and use. If red plums are not available, use yellow plums, greengages or apricots instead.

175 g (6 oz) plain flour
125 g (4 oz) butter, cut into pieces
25 g (1 oz) caster sugar
1 egg yolk
cold water, to mix
Filling:
40 g (1½ oz) ratafias or macaroons
1 kg (2 lb) red plums, quartered and pitted
6 tablespoons plum jam, warmed
150 ml (¼ pint) whipping cream, whipped

Grease a 24 cm (9½ inch) loose-base fluted flan tin. Place the flour in a bowl, add the butter and rub in finely with the fingertips. Stir in the sugar, egg yolk and enough cold water to mix to a firm dough.

Knead the dough on a lightly floured board until smooth. Roll out to a round large enough to line the prepared tin. Press the pastry into the base and fluted sides, then trim off the surplus with a knife. Prick the base with a fork and chill in the refrigerator until firm.

Reserve 18 ratafias for decoration, crush the remainder finely and sprinkle evenly over the base of the flan case. Arrange the quartered plums, overlapping them in circles, around the flan case until it is filled and firmly packed.

Bake in the centre of a preheated oven, 200°C (400°F), Gas Mark 6, for 40–45 minutes until the plums are tender and the pastry is pale golden. Leave the flan until cold in the tin, then carefully remove and place on a serving plate. Spoon the plum jam over the plums to cover and glaze them evenly.

Place the whipped cream in a piping bag, which has been fitted with a small star nozzle.

When the plum jam glaze is cold, lightly mark the top of the flan evenly into 6 wedges with a knife. Pipe a zig-zag of cream from the centre to the edge on each marked line, and then a swirl of cream in between each. Arrange 2 ratafias at the edge of each cream zig-zag and one at each centre end.

Makes one 24 cm (9½ inch) tart

left: German torte
above: *Scandinavian plum tart*

Tipsy French Ring

250 g (8 oz) plain flour

1 teaspoon salt

1 teaspoon caster sugar

1½ teaspoons fast-action dried yeast

3 tablespoons warm water

3 eggs

125 g (4 oz) unsalted butter, softened
and cut into small pieces

Syrup:

175 g (6 oz) sugar

300 ml (½ pint) water

125 ml (4 fl oz) dark rum

To decorate:

2 nectarines, sliced

75 g (3 oz) black grapes, deseeded

75 g (3 oz) white grapes, deseeded

2 oranges, peeled and segmented

2 tablespoons Apricot Glaze
   (see page 77)

25 g (1 oz) flaked almonds

Put the flour, salt, sugar, yeast, warm water and eggs in a warm bowl. Mix together thoroughly with a wooden spoon and then beat for 3–4 minutes to form a smooth, elastic batter. Alternatively, mix in an electric mixer using a dough hook or beater for 1–2 minutes.

Sprinkle the butter pieces over the dough, then cover with some clingfilm and leave in a warm place for about 1 hour, or until the dough has doubled in size.

Brush a 23 cm (9 inch) spring-form ring with melted butter and chill in the refrigerator until set.

Beat the dough with a wooden spoon until all the pieces of butter have been mixed in and the dough is smooth. Spoon the mixture into the ring tin as evenly as possible. Cover the top with clingfilm and leave in a warm place for about 1 hour or until the dough has risen almost to the top of the tin.

Bake in the centre of a preheated oven, 200°C (400°F), Gas Mark 6, for 20 minutes until well risen and golden brown. Remove from the tin and cool on a wire rack.

To make the syrup, put the sugar and water in a saucepan and heat gently until the sugar has dissolved. Bring to the boil and boil rapidly for 3 minutes. Allow the syrup to cool, then stir in the rum.

Place on a serving plate and pour some of the syrup over. As the ring absorbs the syrup, add some more. Continue in this way until the ring is saturated with the syrup.

Fill the centre with the prepared fruit and arrange any remaining fruit around the base. Brush the ring with apricot glaze and stick flaked almonds around the top. Serve any leftover syrup separately.

Makes one 23 cm (9 inch) ring cake

Frangipane Tart

250 g (8 oz) plain flour

125 g (4 oz) butter, softened and cut
   into pieces

25 g (1 oz) caster sugar

1 egg yolk

about 2 tablespoons cold water

Filling:

4 tablespoons redcurrant jelly

375 g (12 oz) redcurrants

125 g (4 oz) butter, softened

125 g (4 oz) caster sugar

125 g (4 oz) ground almonds

25 g (1 oz) plain flour

few drops of almond essence

2 eggs

25 g (1 oz) flaked almonds

1 tablespoon Apricot Glaze
   (see page 77)

whipped cream (optional), to
   decorate

Grease a 25 cm (10 inch) loose-bottomed fluted flan tin. Place the flour in a bowl, add the butter and rub in until the mixture resembles fine breadcrumbs. Stir in the sugar, egg yolk, and enough water to mix to a firm dough.

Knead on a floured board until smooth. Roll out to a round large enough to line the prepared flan tin. Press the pastry on to the base and sides of the tin, and then trim off the surplus with a knife. Reserve the trimmings.

Prick the base of the pastry, then spread with the redcurrant jelly. Reserve a few of the redcurrants for decoration if liked, then distribute the remainder over the jam.

Place the butter, sugar, ground almonds, flour, almond essence and eggs in a mixing bowl. Mix together with a wooden spoon and then beat for 1–2 minutes until smooth. Spoon the mixture into the pastry case and level the top.

Roll out the pastry trimmings and cut into 5 mm (¼ inch) strips. Arrange them in a lattice design over the filling and trim the edges. Position the flaked almonds on the exposed filling in between the lattice, then bake in a preheated oven, 180°C (350°F), Gas Mark 4, for 50–60 minutes until golden brown and firm to the touch. Leave to cool.

When cold, brush the top of the tart with apricot glaze and pipe swirls of cream (if using) around the top. Place one of the reserved redcurrants (if using) on each swirl of cream just before serving.

Makes one 25 cm (10 inch) tart

Making a pastry lattice: Knead the pastry trimmings together and then roll out thinly to make a long thin strip, about 25 x 10 cm (10 x 4 inches). Cut the pastry into 5mm (¼ inch) strips and place half of the strips across the top of the flan, evenly spaced apart. Arrange the remaining strips in the opposite direction and press the pastry strips on to the edge of the tin to trim.

left: tipsy French ring
above: frangipane tart

Marron Tuile Gâteau

125 g (4 oz) plain flour

125 g (4 oz) icing sugar, sifted

2 eggs, separated

4 tablespoons milk

1 teaspoon vanilla essence

300 ml (½ pint) double cream

250 g (8 oz) chestnut purée

3 oranges

25 g (1 oz) pistachio nuts, skinned
    and chopped

Put the flour, icing sugar, egg yolks, milk and vanilla essence in a bowl. Mix together with a wooden spoon, then beat to form a smooth batter. Whisk the egg whites in a clean, dry bowl until stiff, and then fold gently but thoroughly into the batter with a large metal spoon.

Trace eight 9 cm (3½ inch) circles onto a baking sheet lined with nonstick baking paper. Spread a level tablespoon of the mixture on each, then bake in a preheated oven, 180°C (350°F), Gas Mark 4, for 5 minutes. Quickly loosen each round with a palette knife and return to the oven for 2–3 minutes until golden brown at the edges.

Working quickly, roll each round into a cone shape and carefully insert the pointed end of each into a wire rack, so that they will cool standing away from the rack.

Line the baking sheet with a fresh piece of nonstick baking paper and draw three 20 cm (8 inch) circles on it. Spread the remaining mixture over them. Bake for 10–15 minutes until golden brown at the edges. Cool on the paper before removing.

Whip the cream until it is stiff. Reserve 2 tablespoons, then fold the chestnut purée into the remaining cream. Halve 1 orange and cut half into 7 thin wedges. Peel, segment and chop the remaining oranges.

Place one tuile layer on a serving plate. Spread with one-quarter of the chestnut cream and half of the chopped oranges. Top with another layer and cover with chestnut cream and oranges as before. Place the remaining tuile layer on top and spread with chestnut cream.

Place the remaining chestnut cream in a piping bag, fitted with a medium star nozzle. Pipe into each cone and arrange them on top of the gâteau, radiating out from the centre. Add a swirl of chestnut cream in the middle.

Use the remaining cream to pipe a swirl at the end of each cone, and one in the centre. Sprinkle a few pistachio nuts over the cream. Arrange orange wedges in between the cones.

Makes one 20 cm (8 inch) round gâteau

Making tuile cones: Ensure the mixture is spread thinly over each marked circle and cook until it is just beginning to turn a pale gold. Remove the baking sheet and loosen each tuile round from the paper, then return to the oven to soften for a few minutes. Quickly remove only one tuile round at a time and form into a cone shape.

above: marron tuile gâteau
right: Austrian meringue basket

Austrian Meringue Basket

6 egg whites

¾ teaspoon cream of tartar

425 g (14 oz) caster sugar

600 ml (1 pint) double or whipping
  cream

3 tablespoons brandy or sherry

40 g (1½ oz) ratafia biscuits, crushed

375 g (12 oz) strawberries, sliced

375 g (12 oz) raspberries

sugar-frosted flowers (see page 90) or
  crystallized rose petals

Line 4 baking sheets with nonstick baking paper and draw an 18 cm (7 inch) circle on each. Place 4 egg whites and half a teaspoon of cream of tartar in a bowl. Whisk until very stiff, and then gradually whisk in 300 g (10 oz) sugar. Whisk well after each addition until the meringue is thick and stands in peaks.

Place the meringue in a piping bag, which is fitted with a 1 cm (½ inch) plain nozzle. Pipe 2 rings of meringue on the circles on 2 baking sheets and place on the second and third shelves of a preheated oven, 110°C (225°F), Gas Mark ¼.

Pipe another 2 rings of meringue onto the marked circles on the remaining 2 baking sheets, but continue piping to give closed coils, ending in the centre. These will be the basket's lid and base.

Pipe a second ring on top of the outer ring of the base layer and place in the oven with the 2 rings.

Bake the meringues for 20 minutes or until firm enough to lift.

Loosen the 2 circles from the paper. Pipe a few dots of meringue at intervals around the top edge of the base and place one ring on top. Pipe dots on to the ring and place the second ring on top.

Return to the oven with the lid and bake for 20 minutes. Remove the basket and spread the remaining meringue smoothly over the sides. Return to the oven for 20 minutes.

Use the remaining egg whites, cream of tartar and sugar to make some more meringue in the same way. Place this in a piping bag, fitted with a small star nozzle.

Remove the basket from the oven and pipe a double row of scrolls around the top and base of the basket. Remove the lid and return to the oven. Pipe the remaining

meringue in scrolls around the edge and over the top of the lid. Return to the oven for 45–60 minutes until the mixture has set. Leave on the paper until cold.

Whip the cream and brandy or sherry together until thick. Fold in the ratafias and fruit until evenly blended. Place the basket on a flat serving plate and then fill with the fruit and cream mixture. Place the lid in position.

Use whipped cream to attach the sugar-frosted flowers or crystallized rose petals securely to the side and lid of the basket.

Makes one 18 cm (7 inch) basket

Novelty Cakes

Sugar Plum Fairy Castle

6-egg quantity Whisked Sponge Cake
    mixture (see page 79)
6 tablespoons Apricot Glaze
    (see page 77)
1½ quantities Decoration Icing
    (see page 73)
pink food colouring
1-egg quantity Quick Mix Cake
    mixture (see page 80)
425 g (14 oz) sugar
2 teaspoons cold water
cornflour, for sprinkling
30 cm (12 inch) round cake
    board
pink food colouring pen
25 g (1 oz) sugared almonds

Place two-thirds of the whisked sponge mixture in a greased, lined 33 x 23 cm (13 x 9 inch) Swiss roll tin, and the rest in a greased, lined 8 x 12 cm (11 x 7 inch) Swiss roll tin. Bake in a preheated oven, 180°C (350°F), Gas Mark 4, for 15–20 minutes until well risen.

Use some of the apricot glaze as a filling and roll up both Swiss rolls, but roll the smaller Swiss roll lengthways to make a long thin roll.

Make the decoration icing and tint it very pale pink with a few drops of food colouring, then wrap it in clingfilm.

Put the quick mix cake mixture in a greased, lined 20 cm (8 inch) sandwich tin and then bake in a preheated oven, 180°C (350°F), Gas Mark 4, for 15–20 minutes until well risen and firm to the touch. Turn out and cool on a wire rack.

Place the sugar in a bowl, adding a drop of pink food colouring to tint it the same colour as the decoration icing. Reserve one-third of the sugar and add the water to the remainder. Mix well together so that the sugar becomes damp.

Make 3 cone shapes out of greaseproof paper. Fill the large cone with the dampened sugar and press firmly down. Place a piece of card over the top and invert the sugar cone, then remove the paper shape. Repeat to make 1 medium and 2 small cones and leave in a warm place to dry hard.

Trim the ends of each Swiss roll, so that they are level. Cut one-third off each roll to make 4 towers, all of different heights.

Unwrap the decoration icing and cut into 5 pieces. Roll out one piece thinly on a surface well sprinkled with cornflour, the width of the largest roll and long enough to roll completely around it. Brush the roll with some of the remaining apricot glaze, place it on the decoration icing, trim the icing to fit, then roll up, carefully sealing the join well by rubbing over it with cornfloured fingers. Cover the remaining rolls in the same way. Knead and re-roll the trimmings.

Place the reserved sugar on some greaseproof paper. Roll each iced roll in it to coat evenly; leave to dry.

Place the round cake on the cake board and, using plain cutters the same size as the base of each roll, cut out and remove 4 rounds.

Brush the cake with some more of the apricot glaze and roll out the remaining decoration icing to a circle large enough to cover the round cake. Place the icing over the cake, and gently press it into the holes. Smooth over and trim off the excess at the base. Sprinkle the icing and cake board with the remaining pink-tinted sugar.

Place each pink tower in position in the cut-out holes and carefully place the sugar cones on top of each. Make the windows and doors for the towers with the decoration icing trimmings (as illustrated) and use the pink pen to mark the lattice work and door panels. Place these in position and secure with the remaining apricot glaze. Arrange the sugared almonds as a path and steps into the castle.

Makes one fairy castle cake

right: sugar plum fairy castle

Treasure Island

3-egg quantity Quick Mix Cake
  mixture (see page 80)
25 cm (10 inch) thin round cake
  board
1 quantity Fudge Frosting
  (see page 74)
2 tablespoons demerara sugar
blue and green decorating gels
2 jelly feet
1 jelly crocodile
5 curl biscuits
1 tablespoon dessicated coconut
50 g (2 oz) Marzipan (see page 71)
green food colouring
5 pieces Swiss milk chocolate with
  soft filling
milk chocolate coins
jelly sweets

gold and silver almonds
2.5 cm (1 inch) square rice paper
black food colouring pen

Put the cake mixture in a greased
and lined 28 x 18 cm (11 x 7 inch)
oblong tin, 4 cm (1½ inches) deep
and bake in a preheated oven,
170°C (325°F), Gas Mark 3, for
40–45 minutes until well risen and
firm to the touch. Turn out, remove
the paper and cool on a wire rack.

Cut pieces out of the cake to give
it an island shape and place on the
cake board. Reserve the pieces.

Spread about two-thirds of the
fudge frosting evenly all over the
top and sides of the cake. Spread the
remaining cake pieces with frosting
and arrange around and on top of
the cake to resemble rocks.

Sprinkle the demerara sugar
around the cake board and over
the rocks at the base of the cake.
Squeeze the blue gel onto the
remaining cake board to make
the sea.

Squeeze some green gel over the
rocks by the sea edge for seaweed.
Place the jelly feet as footprints in
the sand and position the crocodile
in the sea.

Press the curl biscuits into the top
of the cake by the rocks to make
tree trunks. Colour the coconut
green with a few drops of food
colouring, and then spoon the
coconut mixture round the trees.

Colour the marzipan green with
food colouring and mould 15–18
palm leaves and snip the sides with
a pair of scissors. Gently push

2 or 3 leaves into the top of each tree trunk to attach them firmly.

Using a little fudge frosting, stick 4 pieces of chocolate together to make a chest and then press into the centre of the cake. Place the remaining piece of chocolate resting at the side for a lid. Fill the chest with the chocolate coins, jelly sweets and almonds and press some extras into the cake. Make a map out of rice paper, using the food colouring pen.

Makes one treasure island cake

Good Luck in your New Job

2 x 175 g (6 oz) quantity All-in-One Cakes (see page 78) baked in two 28 x 18 cm (11 x 7 inch) Swiss roll tins
8–10 tablespoons apricot jam
30 cm (12 inch) square cake board
1 kg (2 lb) Decoration Icing (see page 73)
brown, yellow and orange food colouring

Sandwich the cakes with some of the jam and place on the cake board. Thinly spread the top and sides with jam.

To make the newspaper, colour 75 g (3 oz) of the decoration icing orange. Roll out and trim to a 20 cm (8 inch) square. Fold in 3 and leave to dry on greaseproof paper.

Colour 50 g (2 oz) decoration icing yellow. Reserve one-quarter and roll the remaining icing into a handle shape. Put half a cocktail stick into each end of the handle and leave to dry overnight.

Colour the remaining icing brown. Roll out and then trim to an oblong, 35 x 30 cm (14 x 12 inches). Cut two 30 x 2.5 cm (12 x 1 inch) straps, and place the rest of the icing over the top and sides of the cake. Place the straps across the cake as shown and press down lightly. Use the back of a knife to mark a line along the centre of the sides of the cake.

Roll out the yellow decoration icing and cut out one 2.5 cm (1 inch) circle. Cut out a keyhole shape from the centre. Also cut out four 4 cm (1½ inch) circles. Cut each in half and shape to form corner pieces as shown. Brush the back of each corner piece and keyhole piece with a little water and then place on the cake.

Roll the yellow icing trimmings and cut into initials. Make 2 small rolls for combination locks. Brush with a little water and place on the cake. Place the newspaper at an angle to the right-hand side of the cake. Using brown food colouring, paint 'Financial Times' and an appropriate message onto the newspaper. Paint screws on each side of the corner pieces and paint the combination numbers onto the locks. Secure the handle to the cake with a cocktail stick.

Makes one briefcase

left: treasure island
below: good luck in your new job

Chess Board

1 x 20 cm (8 inch) square Light Fruit
  Cake (see page 82)
25 cm (10 inch) square cake
  board
4 tablespoons Apricot Glaze
  (see page 77)
750 g (1½ lb) Marzipan
  (see page 71)
1½ quantities Decoration Icing
  (see page 73)
brown and black food colouring

Place the cake on the board and
trim the top if necessary to make it
level. Brush the top and sides with
apricot glaze, and then cover with
the marzipan. Trim, reserving the
trimmings.

Make the decoration icing, then
divide the icing in half and colour
one-half brown with a few drops of
brown food colouring. Leave the
other half cream. Colour the
remaining marzipan with black
food colouring.

Roll out two-thirds of the brown
icing thinly and cut into an oblong
20 x 10 cm (8 x 4 inches). Cut the
oblong into 4 x 2.5 cm (1 inch)
strips, then each strip into 8 squares,
making 32 in all. Knead all the
trimmings together and reserve.
Repeat with the cream icing and
leave until almost set.

Roll out and trim 2 cream and
2 brown strips of decoration icing
the width and length of each side of
the cake and place alternate strips
around the sides. Brush the top of
the cake with apricot glaze. Arrange
alternate squares of brown and
cream icing on top of the cake and
leave to set. Cut out a strip of
brown and cream icing to trim the
top of the edge of the cake.

Make the chessmen from black
marzipan and the trimmings of the
cream icing. Leave to set, and then
arrange them on the appropriate
squares on top of the cake.

Makes one chess board cake

Golf Course

3-egg quantity Quick Mix Cake
  mixture (see page 80)
1 quantity Butter Cream
  (see page 75)
green, brown and black food
  colouring
50 g (2 oz) desiccated coconut
30 cm (12 inch) thin square cake
  board
2 tablespoons light brown soft
sugar
20 chocolate-coated orange sticks
small piece of red paper
1 sweet cigarette
1 tablespoon plain chocolate dots,
  melted
5 curl biscuits
75 g (3 oz) Marzipan (see page 71)

Place the cake mixture in a greased
and lined 28 x 18 cm (11 x 7 inch)
cake tin, 4 cm (1½ inches) deep.
Bake in a preheated oven, 170°C
(325°F), Gas Mark 3, for 40–45

left: chess board
right: golf course

minutes until well risen and firm to the touch. Turn out, then remove the paper and cool on a wire rack.

Make the butter cream and then colour it green. Place the coconut in a polythene bag with a few drops of green food colouring and shake well to colour evenly.

Cut a sloping piece of cake out of the front corner as a bunker. Spread the butter cream icing over the cake to cover it completely, spreading the centre evenly. Cut the spare piece of cake into 3, cover each with icing and arrange around the top of the cake as landscaping.

Place a 10 cm (4 inch) plain cutter in the centre, then carefully sprinkle the coconut all over the top and sides of the cake, keeping the centre clear. This makes the green.

Place the cake on the cake board and sprinkle the sugar over the bunker to cover it evenly. Carefully remove the cutter.

Press the chocolate-coated orange sticks in position round the outside of the cake for fencing. Cut out a flag shape from the red paper, then attach it to the sweet cigarette and position it in the green. Make a hole near the flag with a straw or something slim.

Spread the melted chocolate over the curl biscuits to coat them evenly. Leave until set, and then press into the cake at the back at different angles for tree trunks.

Colour the marzipan green with a few drops of green food colouring. Press out irregular round shapes, fold and press into the tree trunks to represent the leaves.

Roll a tiny ball of plain marzipan and place on the green, then divide the remaining marzipan and colour it grey and brown with some food colouring. Press into different shaped golf clubs (brown marzipan) and a carrying bag (grey marzipan). Leave to set until firm, then place by the green.

Makes one golf course cake

55

Roll out the brown icing and use to cover the cushion and book case pieces. Use a little more to make a rug and trim it with yellow. Mould the slippers out of scraps of yellow decoration icing.

Using a food colouring pen, write the book title on the cover – 'How to Retire Happily', or similar – and assemble the chair and its accessories.

Makes one armchair cake

Happily Retired

3-egg quantity Lemon Quick Mix Cake mixture (see page 80)
1 quantity Decoration Icing (see page 73)
yellow and brown food colouring
2 tablespoons Apricot Glaze (see page 77)
25 cm (10 inch) thin round cake board
black food colouring pen

Place the cake mixture in a greased, lined 26 x 16 cm (10½ x 7½ inch) oblong cake tin, 5 cm (2 inches) deep. Bake the cake in a preheated oven 170°C (325°F), Gas Mark 3, for 50–55 minutes until well risen and firm to the touch. Turn out, remove the paper and cool on a wire rack.

Make the decoration icing, then colour two-thirds of it streaky yellow by kneading until coloured in streaks, and one-third brown with a few drops of the appropriate food colourings.

Cut the cake according to the diagram (see page 95) and assemble like a chair. Use the cake trimmings to cut out a small cushion and a book. Brush the back and seat pieces with some apricot glaze and press together. Place on the cake board. Roll out about one-third of the yellow icing, large enough to cover the seat, front and back of the chair. Place the icing over the cake, then press into position and trim to fit. Press the trimmings together.

Roll out another third of the icing and cut out 4 side arm pieces, using the cake shape as a template. Brush the outside of the arm pieces with glaze and press the icing on to each side, then brush the top of the arm pieces with apricot glaze. Press the arm pieces into position. Roll out 2 long strips of yellow icing to cover the top of each, press into position and trim.

A Country Cottage

This cake could also be made with a rich fruit cake mixture, covered with marzipan and royal or decoration icing.

1 x 23 cm (9 inch) square All-in-One Cake (see page 78)
4–5 tablespoons raspberry jam
25 cm (10 inch) square cake board
2 quantities Butter Icing (see page 73)
green, brown, pink and yellow food colouring
50 g (2 oz) desiccated coconut
8 shredded wheat biscuits

Cut the cake into 2 halves (oblongs). Trim triangular wedges from 2 long sides of 1 oblong to make a roof and place on top of the other oblong. Sandwich together with jam.

Place the cake to one side of the cake board and cover the top and sides of the cake with butter icing.

Divide the remaining butter icing into 4 small basins and colour it green, brown, pink and yellow. Place each colour in a greaseproof paper piping bag and snip off the ends. Using the brown icing, pipe 4 windows and a door onto the front of the cottage and pipe a winding stone path from the front door to the edge of the board.

With green icing, pipe a rose tree around the door and over the window, using pink icing to pipe dots for roses around the door and a few around the base of the cottage. Spread the remaining green icing thinly over the cake board. Colour the coconut green and scatter over the board, taking care not to cover the path.

Split 4 shredded wheat biscuits in half and then place on the roof as shown. Cut the remaining biscuits into 4 strips and cut each strip in half. Cut 1 strip across its width and place 1 piece over the door of the cottage. Place the remaining strips around the edge of the board as a

fence and secure with icing if necessary. Using yellow and pink icings, pipe little flowers amongst the grass.

Makes one country cottage cake

left: happily retired
below: a country cottage

With Love
to Mum

2-egg quantity 18–20 cm (7–8 inch)
   round Whisked Sponge Cake
   (see page 79)

3 tablespoons lemon curd

300 ml (½ pint) double cream with
   vanilla essence and icing sugar to
   taste or Vanilla Butter Cream
   (see page 75)

primroses and daffodils
   (see page 91)

Sandwich the cake with lemon curd. Place on a pretty serving plate or cake board.

Put the double cream (if using) in a small basin and lightly whip until it just holds its shape. Spread the top of the cake with half-whipped cream or butter cream.

Using a round-ended knife or small palette knife, swirl the cream from the centre outwards in a circular pattern. Put the remaining cream or butter cream in a piping bag, fitted with a medium star nozzle. Pipe a border around the edge of the cake and decorate the centre with primroses, leaves and daffodils. Store in the refrigerator for up to 2 days.

Makes one round flower cake

below: with love to Mum
right: Dad's favourite brew

Dad's Favourite Brew

3-egg quantity All-in-One Cake
  mixture – omit baking powder
  (see page 78)
1 quantity Vanilla Butter Icing
  (see page 73)
1 quantity Chocolate Butter Icing
  (see page 73)
18 cm (7 inch) round cake board
¼ quantity Decoration Icing
  (see page 73) or thin cardboard
2 cocktail sticks

Line the base and grease the sides of
2 clean, dry 250 g (8 oz) coffee tins,
or two 12.5 cm (5 inch) greased and
lined cake tins. Divide the cake
mixture between the tins and bake
in a preheated oven, 180°C (350°F),
Gas Mark 4, for 35–40 minutes.
When cooked, the cakes should feel
firm to the touch and have begun
to shrink from the sides of the tins.
Turn out onto a wire rack and allow
to cool.

To decorate the cake, with a sharp
knife cut a 2.5 cm (1 inch) thick
slice from the top of one cake and
then cut into a handle shape.
Sandwich the remaining cakes
together with half of the vanilla
butter icing and place on the centre
of the cake board.

Reserve 3 tablespoons chocolate
butter icing and spread the rest of
the butter icing carefully onto the
side of the cake and handle. Place
the handle against the side and

secure with cocktail sticks. Roughly
spread the remaining vanilla butter
icing on top of the cake, allowing a
little to spill down the sides.

Roll out the decoration icing and
cut out an oval plaque, or cut one
out from the cardboard. Place the
remaining chocolate butter icing in
a greaseproof paper piping bag, snip
off the end with some scissors and

pipe a message onto the plaque.
Position on the side of the cake.

Makes one beer mug cake

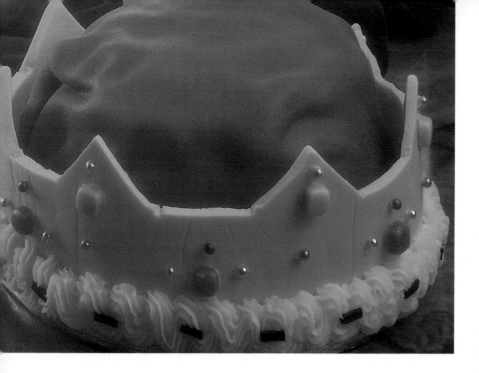

The Royal Crown

175 g (6 oz) self-raising flour

25 g (1 oz) cornflour

1½ teaspoons baking powder

2 tablespoons cocoa powder

3 eggs

175 g (6 oz) caster or light soft brown
   sugar

175 g (6 oz) soft margarine

18–20 cm (7–8 inch) round cake
   board

To decorate:

2 quantities Vanilla Butter Cream
   (see page 75)

375 g (12 oz) Marzipan (see page 71)

yellow and orange liquid food
   colouring and others of your choice

375 g (12 oz) bought fondant icing

a few small brightly coloured sweets

a few silver and coloured balls

small liquorice or chocolate
   matchsticks

Grease a 1 litre (2 pint) ovenproof
pudding basin and dredge with
flour, then knock out the surplus.
Place a disc of greased greaseproof
paper or nonstick baking paper in
the base.

Sift the flour, cornflour, baking
powder and cocoa into a bowl. Add
the eggs, sugar and margarine and
beat gently for about 2 minutes
until smooth. Turn into the basin
and level the top.

Stand the basin on a baking sheet
and bake in a preheated oven,
160°C (325°F), Gas Mark 3, for
about 1 hour or until well risen,
firm to the touch and a skewer
inserted into the centre comes out
clean. Leave to cool in the basin for
1 minute or until the cake begins to
shrink from the sides of the basin,
then turn out on to a wire rack and
leave until cold.

Split the cake horizontally into
2 or 3 pieces, and sandwich back
together again with butter cream.
Stand on a cake board and mask the
whole cake with butter cream.

Colour the marzipan a deep pink,
red, purple or green for the velvet
with some liquid food colouring,
kneading until evenly coloured. Roll
out between 2 sheets of polythene
and use to cover the cake. If wished,
a few creases can be left in as would
be the case with velvet. Trim off any
surplus around the base and then
leave to dry.

Meanwhile, tint the fondant
icing a deep yellow/gold colour
with food colouring. Cut strips of
nonstick baking paper and thick
paper or card long enough to
stretch round the outside of the
cake, about 8.5 cm (3½ inches) deep.

Roll out the icing to a strip long
enough to reach round the cake and
8.5 cm (3½ inches) deep (use 2 strips
if it's easier). Cut out an outline
(copying the photograph), keeping
the main band 5 cm (2 inches) deep
and cutting 7 or 8 points round it.
Bend the card and nonstick baking
paper into a circle and pin in place.
Put the icing round the outside of
this ring and hold in position with
another strip of nonstick baking
paper. Put in a warm place to dry.

When the icing is dry, carefully
remove from the paper and card
and put the ring of icing over the
marzipanned cake. Attach small
pieces of brightly coloured sweets
and silver, gold or coloured balls for
jewels and finally pipe a ruff of
white butter cream around the base
for the ermine. Cut out some small
pieces of liquorice or chocolate
matchsticks and attach them all
round the ermine.

Makes one crown cake

Jigsaw Cat

28–30 cm (11–12 inch) round cake
  board
8-egg quantity lemon or orange
  Madeira Cake mixture
  (see page 81)
3 quantities Butter Cream
  (see page 75)
green, brown, orange and yellow
  liquid food colouring
1 chocolate bean
  (or button)
liquorice or angelica

Grease and line a 25 cm (10 inch) deep round cake tin and spoon in the cake mixture. Bake in a preheated oven, 160°C (325°F), Gas Mark 3, for 1 hour 20 minutes or until well risen, firm to the touch and a skewer inserted in the centre comes out clean. Cool in the tin for

1 minute, then turn out onto a wire rack and leave to go cold.

Peel off the lining paper and then cut out a circle of paper exactly the same size as the cake. Copy the diagram (see page 94) on to the paper. Cut out the jigsaw pieces, then position them on the upside-down cake and cut out the pieces carefully around the paper patterns.

Colour a small amount of the butter cream green (for the eyes) and a small amount dark brown or black (for the nose and centre of the eyes). Colour the remaining butter cream gingery orange.

Carefully number the pieces of cake according to the pattern, with small pieces of numbered paper, then spread green butter cream over the top of numbers 5 and 6 for the eyes – do not cover the sides. Then cover the top of number 7 (nose) with dark brown butter cream.

Put the orange butter cream into a piping bag, fitted with a star nozzle, and pipe stars all over the tops of all the other pieces.

Very carefully, reassemble the jigsaw to form a cat on a round cake board, making the pieces just touch. Then, with the same piping bag and orange icing, continue to pipe stars all over the outside pieces of cake.

Complete the eyes with a dark butter cream. Position a chocolate bean for a nose. Cut the liquorice or angelica into very narrow strips and attach to the cat for its whiskers and mouth. Leave to set.

Makes one jigsaw cat cake

left: the royal crown
below: jigsaw cat

Mantel Clock

3 quantities 3-egg Quick Mix Cake
   mixture (see page 80)
2 tablespoons coffee essence or
   instant coffee powder
2 tablespoons cocoa powder
1½ quantities Coffee Butter Cream
   (see page 75)
33 x 18 cm (13 x 7 inch) cake
   board
1 quantity Apricot Glaze
   (see page 77)
1.25 kg (2½ lb) white marzipan
brown liquid food colouring
5 chocolate buttons
2 chocolate matchsticks
   (optional)
1 curtain ring, about 2.5–4 cm
   (1–1½ inch)

Make up the cake mixtures, one at a
time, and flavour the first 2 with

1 tablespoon coffee essence or
powder in each. Flavour the third
mixture with the sifted cocoa. Bake
each one in a greased and lined
28 x 18 x 4 cm (11 x 7 x 1½ inch)
tin in a preheated oven at 180°C
(350°F), Gas Mark 4, for 35–40
minutes in each (working in batches
if necessary). Turn out each cake on
to a wire rack and leave to cool.

When the cakes are cold, strip off
the lining paper and sandwich with
some of the butter cream.

Trim off the edges of the cake to
give a neat rectangle and stand the
cake up on a cake board. Attach it
to the board with a little butter
cream and then brush all over with
the apricot glaze.

Reserve about 175 g (6 oz) of the
white marzipan and colour the
remainder a mid-brown, using
brown food colouring. Knead until
the colouring is evenly blended.

Roll out one-quarter of the coloured
marzipan between 2 sheets of
polythene and cut to fit the top of
the cake. Position carefully.

Roll out the remainder and cut
into 2 strips, each about 35 x 18 cm
(14 x 7 inches). Fit 1 strip over the
front of the clock and round one
side, trimming to fit the corner, and
then attach the other piece for the
back and remaining sides.

Roll out the reserved white
marzipan thinly and then cut out a
14 cm (5½ inch) circle. With butter
cream, attach this centrally to the
front of the clock for the face. Also
cut out 2 panels, about 15 x 3.5 cm
(6 x 1¼ inches), to fit down the
front of the clock on either side of
the clock face and position these
with butter cream. To make the
clock face, attach 4 chocolate
buttons with butter cream around
the edge and one in the centre.

Put a little butter cream into a piping bag, fitted with a medium writing nozzle, and write the numbers on the chocolate buttons; then pipe just a small line to represent all the other figures.

For the hands, either use chocolate matchsticks, attaching them with butter cream, or pipe in position with butter cream.

Put some butter cream into a piping bag, fitted with a star nozzle, and pipe a line of shells down the centre of each of the marzipan panels. Pipe stars on the front and sides, and a series of stars in the centre of the top of the clock, working it up into a slight peak. Attach the curtain ring for the handle and leave to dry.

Makes one clock cake

left: mantel clock
above: summer straw hat

Summer Straw Hat

4-egg quantity Quick Mix Cake
   mixture (see page 80)
grated rind of 2 oranges or
   lemons
20 g (¾ oz) cornflour
28 cm (11 inch) round or square cake
   board
125 g (4 oz) jam or lemon curd
2 quantities Vanilla Butter Cream
   (see page 75)
yellow liquid food colouring, or
   another colour
about 1 metre (1 yard) heavy ribbon,
   2.5–4 cm (1–1½ inches) wide
1 artificial flower or 1 red flower or a
   few moulded roses (see page 91)

Grease and base-line a 25 cm (10 inch) round cake or sandwich tin. Grease a 900 ml (1½ pint) basin and dredge with flour. Make up the cake mixture, adding the fruit rind and omitting the vanilla essence. Put about two-thirds of the mixture into the prepared tin and level the top. Beat the cornflour into the remaining mixture and pour into the prepared basin.

Bake the cakes in a preheated oven, 160°C (325°F), Gas Mark 3, for about 40 minutes for the round cake, and about 50 minutes for the basin, or until the cakes are well risen and firm to the touch and a skewer inserted in the centre comes out clean. Turn out on to wire racks and leave to cool.

Stand the round cake on a cake board. Spread the base of the basin cake with jam or lemon curd and stand centrally on the first cake.

Colour the butter cream lightly with yellow food colouring to give a deep shade of cream (or any other colour you like). Beginning in the centre of the hat, work a basket weave pattern (see page 89), using a medium writing nozzle and ribbon or basket nozzle. The size of the weave will have to be adjusted to follow the shape of the hat. Leave to set.

Tie a ribbon (with a strip of nonstick baking paper or some greaseproof paper inside it to prevent grease marks) around the hat and finish with long streamers. Add a large, real or artificial flower or a few moulded roses to the side of the hat.

Makes one hat cake

Castle Cake

25 g (1 oz) cocoa

3 tablespoons hot water

175 g (6 oz) margarine

175 g (6 oz) caster sugar

3 eggs

175 g (6 oz) self-raising flour, sifted

To decorate:

1 quantity Chocolate Butter Icing
  (see page 73)

wafers

wafer-thin chocolate mints

flags and toy soldiers

Line and grease an 18 x 28 cm
(7 x 11 inch) Swiss roll tin, leaving
2.5 cm (1 inch) paper above the
sides. Blend the cocoa with the hot
water, and cool slightly. Cream the
margarine and sugar until light and
fluffy, then beat in the cocoa.

Beat in the eggs, one at a time,
adding a tablespoon of the flour
with the last two. Fold in the
remaining flour and turn into the
prepared tin. Bake in a preheated
oven, 190°C (375°F), Gas Mark 5,
for 25–30 minutes. Turn out onto a
wire rack to cool.

Cut a 3.5 cm (1½ inch) strip from
one end of the cake and cut into
4 squares. Cut the remaining cake
in half and sandwich together with
the icing. Cover the top and sides of
the cake with icing. Smooth and
then mark lines for bricks. Cover
the squares with the remaining
icing and place them on the corners
for turrets.

Cut the wafers to make windows
and a door and place in position.
Cut the mints into small squares
and place between the turrets for
battlements. Finish with flags at
each corner and toy soldiers.

Makes one castle cake

above: castle cake
right: Dennis dinosaur

Dennis Dinosaur

2-egg quantity Quick Mix Cake
  mixture (see page 80)
peppermint essence
green food colouring
1 quantity Decoration Icing
  (see page 73)
2 tablespoons Apricot Glaze
  (see page 77)
2 mini chocolate Swiss rolls
3 sweet cigarettes
red dragees
2 strips strawberry flavour liquorice

Grease and base-line a 20 cm
(8 inch) round sandwich tin. Make
the cake mixture according to the
instructions, adding a few drops of
peppermint essence and green food
colouring. Put the mixture in the
prepared tin and then bake in a
preheated oven, 160°C (325°F), Gas

Mark 3, for 40–45 minutes until
well risen and firm to the touch.
Turn out the cake, remove the paper
and cool on a wire rack.

Make the decoration icing and
colour it green with food colouring.

Using a 7.5 cm (3 inch) plain
cutter, cut a round out from the
centre of the cake and remove. Cut
the cake into 2 half-circles and
sandwich together with some of the
apricot glaze (see page 95).

Roll out two-thirds of the icing
and cover the cake completely,
carefully sealing the joins
underneath the arched body shape.

Cut the mini Swiss rolls in half to
make 4 legs and cut the remaining
round piece of cake in half. Use
one-half for a head, then cut the
other semi-circle in half for the tail
pieces, as in the diagram on page 95.

Roll out the remaining icing and
carefully cover the legs, head and

tail pieces. Leave all the pieces to set
for at least 1 hour in a warm place
or preferably overnight.

Arrange the legs on a long board
or tray and brush the tops with
apricot glaze. Place the body in
position. Press 2 sweet cigarettes
into the head end and one into the
tail end, brush the head and one tail
piece with glaze at one end and
press on to the body. Attach the
remaining tail piece with glaze.

Using red dragees, press into the
head for the eyes and mouth. Cut
the liquorice strips in half, then
into diamond shapes. Press these
into the icing all over the head,
back and tail to represent spines.

Cut the remaining pieces of
liquorice into tiny toe nails and
stick them around the feet with the
remaining apricot glaze.

Makes one dinosaur cake

Football Crazy

4-egg quantity All-in-One Cake
mixture (see page 78), omitting
baking powder and baked in a
25 x 20 cm (10 x 8 inch) roasting tin
for 45–50 minutes

4–5 tablespoons apricot jam

30 cm (12 inch) square cake board

1 quantity Decoration or Gelatine
Icing (see page 73)

blue, yellow, green and black food
colouring

2 liquorice laces

1 quantity Butter Icing
(see page 73)

50 g (2 oz) chocolate dots

50 g (2 oz) desiccated coconut

Split the cake in half and sandwich
with jam. Cut the cake into a boot
and a ball shape and place on the
cake board.

Roll out half of the decoration or
gelatine icing into an oblong large
enough to cover the top and sides
of the boot only. Cover the boot,
cutting away the icing at the ankle.
Roll one-quarter of the remaining
icing into a circle and use to cover
the football.

Using the back of a knife, mark
the top of the football into 5-sided
pentagons. Using an artist's paint
brush and black food colouring,
paint in the central pentagon.
Divide the remaining icing in half,
colour one half blue and roll out.

Cut a patch to cover the angle of
the boot, a strip for the laces and a
flash on the boot.

Colour the remaining icing
yellow, roll out and cut smaller
shapes to go on top of the ankle
patch and flash. Cut liquorice laces
and place on the cake with a bow at
the ankle.

Colour half of the butter icing
blue and the other half yellow.
Using a star nozzle, pipe alternate
coloured stripes for the sock as
shown. Place chocolate dots on the
sole of the boot. Colour the coconut
green and sprinkle over the cake
board for the grass.

Makes one football cake

A Dartmoor Pony

3-egg quantity All-in-One Cake
  mixture (see page 78), baked in
  2 x 23 cm (9 inch) round tins

4–5 tablespoons apricot jam

30 inch (12 inch) round cake board

2 quantities Coffee Butter Icing
  (see page 73)

½ quantity Chocolate Butter Icing
  (see page 73)

3 strips liquorice

liquorice sweets, to decorate

Sandwich the cakes together with jam. Cut out the horse's head and ear as shown on page 95. Place the horse's head on the board. Join the ear to the head with a little butter icing. Spread the cake all over with coffee butter icing.

Mark a line to show the curve of the head against the neck. Put the chocolate butter icing into a greaseproof paper piping bag and snip the end. Pipe the mane along the horse's neck.

Arrange the strips of liquorice on the cake to form a bridle as shown. Pipe the horse's eye, the nostrils and mouth as shown below. Decorate with the liquorice sweets.

Makes one horse's head cake

left: *football crazy*
below: *a Dartmoor pony*

Caterpillar Cake

4-egg quantity Quick Mix Cake
  mixture (see page 80)

1½ quantities Chocolate or Coffee
  Butter Cream (see page 75)

175 g (6 oz) raspberry jam

33 x 18 cm (13 x 7 inch) cake board

1 quantity Marzipan (see page 71)

green, blue and yellow liquid food
  colouring

2 chocolate buttons or beans for eyes

liquorice or angelica for antenna and
  mouth

1 moulded rose bud (see page 90) or
  small artificial flowers

Grease and line a 28 x 18 x 4 cm
(11 x 7 x 1½ inch) rectangular tin.

Turn the cake mixture into the
prepared tin and level the top,
making sure that there is plenty
of the mixture in the corners.
Bake in a preheated oven, 160°C
(325°F) Gas Mark 3, for 45–50
minutes or until well risen,
golden brown and firm to the
touch. Turn out on to a wire rack
and leave until cold, then strip off
the lining paper.

Take a plain 6–7 cm (2½–2¾ inch)
cutter and stamp out 8 rounds of
cake. Cut out another half round
for the head from the trimmings.
Sandwich the rounds together with
a little butter cream and the jam
and place on the cake board in a
wavy caterpillar shape, angling the
pieces round to do so.

Remove a small piece of the
marzipan and colour the remainder
bright green, using green and blue
liquid colourings, and then knead
until evenly blended. Roll out the
coloured marzipan thinly between
2 sheets of polythene to a rectangle,
about 10 cm (4 inches) longer than
the caterpillar and wide enough to
go right round it.

Spread the cake all over with a
thin layer of butter cream, and then
carefully lay the marzipan over to
cover it completely. Mould the
marzipan so that it dips between
the sections of the body and fits
neatly over the head and tail. Trim
off any surplus marzipan and fold
the ends under the body.

Tint the remaining butter cream
yellow and put into a piping bag,
fitted with a star nozzle. Pipe a thin
continuous zig-zag line down the
length of the body along its back.

Attach the chocolate buttons for
eyes with butter cream. Cut out
2 antennae and a mouth from the
angelica or liquorice and position
on the head, attaching with butter
cream. Use the butter cream to
make dots all over the body.

Mould the remaining yellow
marzipan into a hat and stick it on
to the caterpillar at a jaunty angle.
Add the moulded rose or artificial
flowers. Leave to dry.

Makes one caterpillar cake

above: caterpillar cake
right: mermaid cake

Mermaid Cake

The mermaid's tail can be coloured in shades of pink, mauve or yellow, if preferred. This design can also be used as a fish by itself. Omit the doll and add piped features (or pieces of liquorice) on the fish's head.

2-egg quantity Quick Mix Cake, any flavour (see page 80) baked in a 28 x 18 x 4 cm (11 x 7 x 1½ inch) tin for 40 minutes

28 cm (11 inch) square cake board

small doll with long hair (without legs)

a little white lace and/or ribbon

1 quantity Apricot Glaze (see page 77)

500 g (1 lb) bought fondant icing

green and blue liquid food colouring

icing sugar and cornflour, for dredging

1 quantity Butter Cream (see page 75)

silver balls (optional)

Take a piece of paper, the same size as the cake, and draw the outline of a fish's body and tail on it. Position on top of the cake and cut out, making the tail fin from the cake trimmings.

Assemble the whole fish on a cake board. Take the doll and make a bodice with the lace and/or ribbon. Set the doll into the cake, cutting out a piece of cake if necessary and trimming it to fit round the body. Brush the cake all over with apricot glaze.

Divide the fondant icing into quarters and colour one piece a very pastel blue, a second a deep blue, a third a pale green/blue, and the last a deeper blue/green. Knead each piece until it is evenly coloured.

Roll out each piece of fondant icing thinly between 2 sheets of polythene or on a surface dredged with a mixture of icing sugar and cornflour. From the rolled-out icing, cut out circles of about 2.5–4 cm (1–1½ inches) with a plain cutter.

Beginning at the tail, arrange lines of these circles to cover the cake, representing the scales of a fish. Keep the paler colours mainly near the doll and begin with the darker ones at the tail end. Tuck the edges of the circle under the cake.

Pipe a row of butter cream shells round the waist of the doll to attach it to the cake and a row around the base of the scales to attach the cake to the board. Wavy lines of shells can be piped on to the board to represent the waves on the sea. A few silver balls can also be attached at random to the fish scales with some small dabs of butter cream.

Makes one mermaid cake

Basic Recipes

Icings, Coverings and Fillings

Quantity Chart for Marzipan

These quantities are sufficient for marzipanning a whole cake – to marzipan the top only, halve the quantities given.

Square tin							
12 cm (5 inch)	15 cm (6 inch)	18 cm (7 inch)	20 cm (8 inch)	23 cm (9 inch)	25 cm (10 inch)	28 cm (11 inch)	30 cm (12 inch)
Round tin							
15 cm (6 inch)	18 cm (7 inch)	20 cm (8 inch)	23 cm (9 inch)	25 cm (10 inch)	28 cm (11 inch)	30 cm (12 inch)	33 cm (13 inch)
Apricot glaze							
1½ tablespoons	2 tablespoons	2½ tablespoons	3 tablespoons	3½ tablespoons	4 tablespoons	4½ tablespoons	5 tablespoons
Marzipan							
500 g (1 lb)	750 g (1½ lb)	875 g (1¾ lb)	1 kg (2 lb)	1.25 kg (2½ lb)	1.5 kg (3 lb)	1.75 kg (3½ lb)	2 kg (4 lb)

Marzipan

Marzipan is used for covering cakes to give a smooth, flat surface before applying royal icing or ready-to-roll icing. Take care not to over-knead the marzipan as handling it too much encourages the oils from the ground almonds to flow and eventually seep through the iced surface of the cake, staining it. Ready-made marzipan is available in white and yellow.

250 g (8 oz) ground almonds
125 g (4 oz) caster sugar
125 g (4 oz) icing sugar, sifted
1 teaspoon lemon juice
few drops of almond flavouring
1 egg or 1 large egg white
sifted icing sugar, for dusting

Place the ground almonds, caster and icing sugars in a bowl. Stir until evenly mixed. Make a well in the centre and then add the lemon juice, almond flavouring and enough beaten egg or egg white to mix to a soft but firm dough.

Lightly dust a work surface with sifted icing sugar and knead the marzipan until it is smooth and free from cracks. Wrap in clingfilm or store in a polythene bag until ready for use. Tint with food colouring if required, and use for moulding or covering cakes.

Makes 500 g (1 lb) marzipan

Royal Icing

This traditional icing is used to cover many celebration cakes – according to the consistency, it may be used for flat icing, peaked icing or even piping designs on to cakes.

2 egg whites
¼ teaspoon lemon juice
500 g (1 lb) icing sugar, sifted
1 teaspoon glycerine

Makes 500 g (1 lb) royal icing

Quantity Chart for Royal Icing

Quantity	Cake size
500 g (1 lb)	12 cm (5 inch) square
	15 cm (6 inch) round
750 g (1½ lb)	15 cm (6 inch) square
	18 cm (7 inch) round
1 kg (2 lb)	18 cm (7 inch square)
	20 cm (8 inch) round
1.25 kg (2½ lb)	20 cm (8 inch) square
	23 cm (9 inch) round
1.5 kg (3 lb)	23 cm (9 inch) square
	25 cm (10 inch) round
1.75 kg (3½ lb)	25 cm (10 inch) square
	28 cm (11 inch) round
2 kg (4 lb)	28 cm (11 inch) square
	30 cm (12 inch) round
2.25 kg (4½ lb)	30 cm (12 inch) square
	33 cm (13 inch) round

1 Stir the egg whites and lemon juice together and then mix in some of the icing sugar.

2 Keep adding icing sugar, mixing well after each addition. Stir in the glycerine until well blended.

3 Cover the surface with some damp clingfilm. Stir thoroughly before using to disperse the air bubbles; adjust the consistency if necessary.

Meringue Icing

Lightly cooked meringue combined with softly beaten butter makes an icing similar to crème au beurre but less rich, using egg whites instead of egg yolks. The meringue should be whisked in a heatproof bowl suspended over a pan of simmering, not boiling, water. All the flavourings are suitable for coating and filling but textured flavourings are not suitable for piping.

2 egg whites
125 g (4 oz) icing sugar, sifted
150 g (5 oz) unsalted butter, softened

Covers and fills a 20 cm (8 inch) sandwich cake

Flavourings
• **Citrus:** Add 2 teaspoons finely grated orange, lemon or lime rind.
• **Chocolate:** Add 50 g (2 oz) plain chocolate, melted.
• **Coffee:** Add 2 teaspoons instant coffee granules blended with 1 teaspoon boiling water, cooled.
• **Vanilla:** Add a few drops of vanilla essence.
• **Almond:** Add a few drops of almond essence.
• **Nut:** Add 25 g (1 oz) nuts, finely chopped and toasted. Toasting the nuts brings out their flavour.
• **Caramel:** Add 25 g (1 oz) crushed caramel (see page 77).
• **Praline:** Add 25 g (1 oz) crushed praline.

1 Whisk the egg whites until frothy. Gently beat in the icing sugar and then place the bowl over a saucepan of simmering water. Whisk until the meringue is thick and white.

3 Using a wooden spoon or spatula, if wished, fold in the flavouring of your choice, e.g. orange rind, until evenly blended. Use immediately.

2 Remove from the heat and whisk until the meringue is cool and it stands up in soft peaks. Add the meringue gradually to the butter, beating well after each addition.

Fondant Icing

375 g (12 oz) icing sugar, sifted
1 egg white
1 tablespoon liquid glucose, warmed

Place the icing sugar, egg white and glucose in a bowl and mix, using a palette knife, until a dough is formed. Knead lightly until smooth on a surface which has been lightly dusted with some icing sugar. Wrap the fondant icing in some clingfilm or store it in a polythene bag until needed.

Makes 425 g (14 oz)

Glacé Icing

250 g (8 oz) icing sugar
2–3 tablespoons hot water

Sift the icing sugar into a bowl. Using a wooden spoon, gradually stir in enough hot water until the mixture is the consistency of thick cream. Beat until white and smooth and the icing thickly coats the back of the spoon.

Colour the icing with a few drops of food colouring, if desired. Use the glacé icing immediately to pour over a cake.

Covers the top of a 20 cm (8 inch) round cake

Flavourings
• **Coffee:** Replace the water with strong coffee.
• **Chocolate:** Sift 2 teaspoons cocoa powder with the icing sugar.
• **Citrus:** Replace the water with orange, lemon or lime juice.

Decoration Icing

Use this icing for covering cakes or modelling animals, figures, flowers and leaves. Decoration icing can be coloured and flavoured with food colourings and essences, if wished.

500 g (1 lb) icing sugar
1 large egg white
I rounded tablespoon glucose syrup

Sift the icing sugar. Put the egg white and glucose syrup in a clean, grease-free bowl. Add the icing sugar gradually and mix with a wooden spoon. Turn out onto a work surface and knead in all the icing sugar until the mixture binds together to form a ball.

Covers a 20 cm (8 inch) cake

Gelatine Icing

This icing can be used in the same way as decoration icing, although it does become quite brittle as it dries. Use it for covering cakes and for making cut-out and moulded decorations.

2 tablespoons cold water
2 teaspoons gelatine
1 teaspoon glycerine
500 g (1 lb) icing sugar
1 large egg white

Measure 2 tablespoons of cold water into a small basin and sprinkle in the gelatine. Stand the basin in a saucepan of water over a gentle heat. Stir until the gelatine has completely dissolved and the liquid runs clear. Remove from the heat and stir in the glycerine.

Sift the icing sugar into a bowl and add the egg white and gelatine mixture. Stir well until firm, then knead with the fingers, adding extra icing sugar if necessary to form a smooth pliable paste. Add colouring and flavouring as desired, with extra icing sugar if necessary. Wrap the icing in clingfilm or a polythene bag until required.

Covers a 20 cm (8 inch) cake

Butter Icing

A versatile, quickly made icing which may be flavoured, coloured, spread smoothly, textured with a knife or piped into many designs.

125 g (4 oz) unsalted butter, softened
250 g (8 oz) icing sugar, sifted
2 teaspoons milk
1 teaspoon vanilla essence

Beat the butter in a bowl, using a wooden spoon, until it is light and fluffy. Stir in the icing sugar, milk and vanilla essence. Beat well until light and smooth. Use to cover the top and sides of an 18 cm (7 inch) sandwich cake.

Flavourings
• **Citrus:** Replace the milk and vanilla essence with orange, lemon or lime juice and 2 teaspoons finely grated orange, lemon or lime rind.
• **Chocolate:** Add 1 tablespoon cocoa powder blended with 1 tablespoon boiling water. Set aside to cool before using.
• **Coffee:** Add 2 teaspoons instant coffee granules which have been blended with 1 teaspoon boiling water. Leave to cool before using.

Fudge Frosting

A rich butterscotch-flavoured frosting for quickly coating any sponge cake

75 g (3 oz) unsalted butter
3 tablespoons milk
25 g (1 oz) soft light brown sugar
1 tablespoon black treacle
375 g (12 oz) icing sugar, sifted

Put the butter, milk, sugar and black treacle in a heatproof bowl over a saucepan of simmering water, stirring occasionally with a wooden spoon until the butter has melted and the sugar has dissolved.

Remove the bowl from the saucepan and stir in the icing sugar. Beat until smooth and glossy. Pour immediately over the cake for a smooth finish, or cool for a thicker spreading consistency.

Covers one 18 cm (7 inch) square cake or covers and fills one 20 cm (8 inch) round cake

Flavourings
• **Coffee:** Replace the black treacle with 1 tablespoon instant coffee dissolved in 1 tablespoon boiling water, cooled.
• **Chocolate:** Sift 1 tablespoon cocoa powder with the icing sugar.

American Frosting

This light marshmallow icing crisps on the outside when it is left to dry. It is a versatile frosting which may be swirled into a soft pattern over the top and sides of cakes or used as a filling.

1 egg white
2 tablespoons water
1 tablespoon golden syrup
1 teaspoon cream of tartar
175 g (6 oz) icing sugar, sifted

Place the egg white, water, golden syrup and cream of tartar in a heatproof bowl. Whisk together thoroughly. Stir the icing sugar into the mixture and place the bowl over a saucepan of simmering water.

Whisk until the mixture becomes thick and white. Remove the bowl from the pan and continue to whisk until the mixture is cool and thick and stands up in soft peaks. Use immediately.

Covers a 20 cm (8 inch) round or 18 cm (7 inch) square cake or covers and fills a 20 cm (8 inch) round cake

Butter Cream

125 g (4 oz) unsalted butter
250 g (8 oz) icing sugar, sifted
2 tablespoons milk
flavouring of your choice or a few
    drops of food colouring

Beat the butter with half of the
icing sugar until smooth. Add the
remaining icing sugar with the milk
and any flavouring of your choice.
If stored in an airtight container in
the refrigerator, this will keep for
several weeks.

Makes 375 g (12 oz)

Flavourings
• **Chocolate:** Dissolve 2 tablespoons
cocoa powder in 2 tablespoons boiling
water. Cool and add to the mixture with
only 1 tablespoon milk.
• **Citrus:** Add the grated rind of either
1 lemon, orange or lime with a
tablespoon of juice to the mixture and
only 1 tablespoon milk.
• **Coffee:** Replace 1 tablespoon milk
with 1 tablespoon coffee essence.
• **Vanilla:** Add a few drops of vanilla
essence to the butter cream.

Crème au Beurre

Also known as continental buttercream,
this is a rich but smooth, light-textured
icing suitable for filling, coating or
piping on special cakes and gâteaux.
Use as soon as it is made for the best
results. Do not re-beat or it will curdle.

4 tablespoons water or fruit juice
    (see flavourings right)
75 g (3 oz) caster sugar
2 egg yolks
150 g (5 oz) unsalted butter,
    softened

1 Make the sugar syrup using water
or fruit juice and sugar. Whisk the
egg yolks and continue whisking
while slowly adding the sugar syrup
in a steady stream. Whisk until the
mixture is thick, pale and cool, and
it leaves a trail on the surface when
the beaters are lifted.

Covers a 20 cm (8 inch)
round cake or covers and
fills an 18 cm (7 inch) round
cake

Flavourings
• **Citrus:** Replace the water with orange,
lemon or lime juice and fold in. Add
2 teaspoons finely grated orange, lemon
or lime rind to the finished mixture.
• **Chocolate:** Add 50 g (2 oz) plain dark
chocolate, melted, to the finished
mixture. Mix in well.
• **Coffee:** Fold in 2 teaspoons instant
coffee, dissolved in 1 teaspoon boiling
water, cooled, to the finished mixture.

2 Beat the butter with a wooden
spoon in a separate bowl until it is
light and fluffy. Gradually add the
egg mixture, beating well after each
addition, until the crème au beurre
is thick and fluffy. Use immediately.

Pastry Cream

An alternative filling to cream (also known as crème pâtissière), this may be used to fill gâteaux, cakes and pastries.

2 egg yolks

50 g (2 oz) caster sugar

15 g (½ oz) cornflour

15 g (½ oz) plain flour

300 ml (½ pint) milk

1 tablespoon Marsala or rose or orange flower water

125 ml (4 fl oz) whipped cream (optional)

Makes about 450 ml (¾ pint)

1 In a bowl, whisk the egg yolks and sugar until pale and thick. Mix together the cornflour and plain flour and sift into the egg mixture. Whisk until smooth.

2 Bring the milk to the boil and gradually pour onto the egg mixture, whisking until well blended. Strain through a sieve into a clean pan. Bring slowly to the boil, whisking all the time until the mixture begins to thicken. Cook for 1 minute, whisking until thick and smooth.

3 Add the Marsala or rose or orange flower water, whisking well until blended. Pour into a bowl, cover the top with clingfilm and leave until cold. Use as required. To make a lighter textured filling, fold in some whipped cream and use at once.

Caramel

This is sugar syrup which is boiled to a very high temperature, until the sugar begins to caramelize. When the sugar syrup turns pale golden it has a honey flavour; when it reaches golden brown it is caramel; as it darkens it has the flavour of treacle. Watch the caramel carefully so that it does not burn and taste bitter. Always take care when making and using caramel, as it reaches a very high temperature.

150 ml (¼ pint) water
175 g (6 oz) caster sugar

1 Bring the water to the boil in a heavy-based pan. Remove from the heat and stir in the sugar. Heat gently, stirring occasionally, until the sugar dissolves, then bring to the boil, and boil rapidly until the bubbles subside and the syrup turns golden brown or reaches 154–175°C (310–350°F) on a sugar thermometer.

2 If wished, you can pour the caramel onto some foil which has been lightly brushed with oil. Leave it to go cold and hard before using. Alternatively, you can dip nuts and grapes into the caramel to use as a decoration when cold.

Apricot Glaze

Use when marzipanning cakes, and as a glazing for fruits on gâteaux and cakes.

500 g (1 lb) apricot jam
3 tablespoons water

Put the jam and water in a saucepan and heat gently, stirring occasionally until the jam has melted. Boil rapidly for 1 minute, then strain through a sieve. Rub through as much fruit as possible, using a wooden spoon. Throw away the contents of the sieve. Pour the glaze into a clean, sterilized jar, seal with a clean lid and cool. Refrigerate for up to 2 months.

Sugar Syrup

This is suitable for glazes, brushing the tops of cakes, coating fruits, cooking fruit without breaking the fruit down and as a base for crème au beurre.

125 ml (4 fl oz) water
125 g (4 oz) caster sugar

Bring the water to the boil in a small saucepan. Remove the pan from the heat and stir in the sugar. Replace the pan over the heat and heat gently, stirring occasionally with a wooden spoon, until the sugar is completely dissolved. Remove the wooden spoon from the pan.

Boil rapidly until the mixture becomes syrupy, or until the 'thread stage' is reached – 107°C (225°F) on a sugar thermometer. To test, remove the pan from the heat and place a little syrup on the back of a dry teaspoon. Press a second teaspoon onto the syrup and pull them apart. The syrup should form a fine thread. If not, return the pan to the heat, boil the syrup rapidly and re-test 1 minute later. When the syrup is ready, remove the pan from the heat and use immediately.

Cake mixtures

All-in-One Cake Mix

Preheat the oven to 180°C (350°F), Gas Mark 4. Brush the baking tins or basins with melted fat or oil and then line the bases with greased greaseproof paper.

Put the margarine, sugar, eggs, sifted flour, baking powder and flavourings in a mixing bowl. Mix together with a wooden spoon, then beat for 2–3 minutes until smooth and glossy. (This will only take 1–2 minutes in an electric mixer, or between 30 seconds and 1 minute in a food processor.)

Put the mixture into the prepared tins, level the tops with the back of a spoon and bake in the centre of the preheated oven for the required time. Test the cake by pressing with your fingers. If cooked, it should spring back and just begun to shrink from the sides of the tin. Allow to cool for 5 minutes before loosening the sides of the cake from the tin. Turn out onto a wire rack.

All-in-One Cake Mix Quantities

Basic recipe	Cake tin size	Approx. cooking time
125 g (4 oz) soft tub margarine	two 18 cm (7 inch) sandwich tins	25–30 minutes
125 g (4 oz) caster sugar	one 20 cm (8 inch) sandwich tin	30–35 minutes
2 large eggs	one 18 cm (7 inch) deep square tin	35–40 minutes
125 g (4 oz) self-raising flour	one 20 cm (8 inch) shallow square tln	25–30 minutes
1 teaspoon baking powder	one 0.5 kg (1 lb) loaf tin – omit baking	45–50 minutes
Flavourings	powder	
4 drops vanilla essence	one 900 ml (1½ pint) basin – omit	50–60 minutes
4 teaspoons cocoa	baking powder	
2 teaspoons grated lemon or	one 20 cm (8 inch) ring mould	35–40 minutes
orange rind		
2 teaspoons instant coffee		

Basic recipe	Cake tin size	Approx. cooking time
175 g (6 oz) soft tub margarine	two 20 cm (8 inch) sandwich tins	35–40 minutes
175 g (6 oz) caster sugar	two 23 cm (9 inch) sandwich tins	25 minutes
3 large eggs	one 15 cm (6 inch) deep cake tin	45–50 minutes
175 g (6 oz) self-raising flour	one 18 cm (7 inch) deep square tin	45–50 minutes
½ teaspoon baking powder	one 28 x 18 cm (11 x 7 inch) Swiss	35–40 minutes
Flavourings	roll tin	
6 drops vanilla essence	1.2 litre (2 pint) basin – omit baking	1¼–1½ hours
2 tablespoons cocoa	powder	
1 tablespoon grated lemon or		
orange rind		
1 tablespoon instant coffee		

Basic recipe	Cake tin size	Approx. cooking time
250 g (8 oz) soft tub margarine	one 23 cm (9 inch) round tin – omit	1 hour
250 g (8 oz) caster sugar	baking powder	
4 large eggs	one 23 cm (9 inch) square tin – omit	1 hour
250 g (8 oz) self-raising flour	baking powder	
2 teaspoons baking powder	one 29 x 22 cm (11½ x 8½ inch) Swiss	40 minutes
Flavourings	roll tin	
8 drops vanilla essence		
4 tablespoons cocoa		
2 tablespoons grated lemon or		
orange rind		
2 tablespoons instant coffee		

Whisked Sponge

1 Whisk the eggs and sugar over a pan of simmering water until thick and pale. Remove from the pan and continue whisking until cool. Fold in the sifted flour and flavourings. Pour into a prepared tin and bake.

Whisked Sponge Cake Quantities

Ingredients	Quantity	Quantity	Quantity	Quantity
Eggs	2	3	4	6
Caster sugar	50 g (2 oz)	75 g (3 oz)	125 g (4 oz)	175 g (6 oz)
Plain flour	50 g (2 oz)	75 g (3 oz)	125 g (4 oz)	175 g (6 oz)

2 To test whether the sponge is cooked, press it very lightly in the centre. If it springs back, the cake is cooked. However, if your fingers leave a slight depression in the centre of the cake, it will need some extra cooking time.

3 After removing the cooked cake from the oven, turn it out onto a wire rack and leave to cool. You can do this by placing the rack on top of the cake and then turning the tin over so that the sponge drops out onto the rack without breaking.

Flavourings

These amounts are for a 2-egg quantity of whisked sponge. Increase the suggested flavourings proportionately for the quantity being made.

• **Chocolate:** Replace 15 g (½ oz) flour with the same weight of cocoa powder, or add 25 g (1 oz) plain dark chocolate, melted.

• **Citrus:** Add 2 teaspoons finely grated orange, lemon or lime rind. Unwaxed fruit is best.

• **Coffee:** Add 2 teaspoons instant coffee granules which have been blended with 1 teaspoon boiling water.

• **Nut:** Replace 25 g (1 oz) flour with the same weight of finely ground nuts, such as walnuts or hazelnuts.

Genoese Sponge

4 eggs
125 g (4 oz) caster sugar
100 g (3½ oz) unsalted butter, melted
100 g (3½ oz) plain flour

Flavourings
• **Chocolate:** Add 50 g (2 oz) plain dark chocolate, melted.
• **Citrus:** Add 2 teaspoons finely grated orange, lemon or lime rind.
• **Coffee:** Add 2 teaspoons instant coffee granules dissolved in 1 teaspoon boiling water.

1 Whisk the eggs and sugar in a heatproof bowl. Place over a pan of simmering water and whisk until thick and pale. Remove from the heat and whisk until cool and the mixture leaves a trail when the beaters are lifted. Pour in the butter with a flavouring, if using.

2 Sift the flour over the surface of the mixture and then fold into the mixture with the melted butter. Pour into the prepared tin and then bake in a preheated oven according to the individual recipe.

Quick Mix Cake

Sift the flour and baking powder into a mixing bowl. Mix in the sugar, margarine and eggs. Beat for 1–2 minutes until smooth and glossy. Stir in the chosen flavouring and beat until evenly blended. Pour into the prepared tin and then bake in a preheated oven, 160°C (325°F), Gas Mark 3, for the time specified in the chart (below right).

Note
When recipes are made in a loaf tin, deep mould or pudding basin, omit the baking powder; otherwise the cake may have a depression in the centre when cooked. For a 1-egg quantity, halve the measurements for a 2-egg quantity cake.

Flavourings
These amounts are for a 2-egg quantity. Increase the suggested flavourings to suit the quantity being made.
• **Chocolate:** Add 2 tablespoons cocoa powder combined with 1 tablespoon boiling water, or add 25 g (1 oz) plain dark chocolate, melted, or 25 g (1 oz) chocolate dots.

• **Citrus:** Add 2 teaspoons finely grated orange, lemon or lime rind, preferably from unwaxed fruit.
• **Coffee:** Add 2 teaspoons instant coffee granules which have been blended with 1 teaspoon boiling water.
• **Nut:** Replace 25 g (1 oz) flour with the same weight of finely ground nuts, such as walnuts or hazelnuts.

Quick Mix Cake Quantities

Ingredients	Quantity	Quantity	Quantity
Self-raising flour	125 g (4 oz)	175 g (6 oz)	250 g (8 oz)
Baking powder	1 teaspoon	1½ teaspoons	2 teaspoons
Caster sugar	125 g (4 oz)	175 g (6 oz)	250 g (8 oz)
Soft margarine	125 g (4 oz)	175 g (6 oz)	250 g (8 oz)
Eggs	2	3	4
Approx. cooking time	40–45 minutes	50–55 minutes	1–1¼ hours

Madeira Cake

Grease and line a deep cake tin. Sift the flour and baking powder into a mixing bowl. Add the caster sugar, margarine, eggs and milk or juice. Mix together with a wooden spoon, then beat for 1–2 minutes until smooth and glossy. Alternatively, use an electric mixer and beat for 1 minute only. Add any flavourings, if required, and blend in well.

Spoon the mixture into the prepared tin and spread it evenly. Give the tin a sharp tap to remove any air pockets. Make a depression in the centre to ensure a level surface to the cooked cake.

Bake in the centre of a preheated oven, 160°C (325°F), Gas Mark 3,

for the time specified on the chart, or until the cake springs back when lightly pressed in the centre. Cool slightly in the tin, then remove the cake and cool completely on a wire rack. Wrap in clingfilm or foil and store in a cool place until required.

Flavourings

These quantities are for a 3-egg quantity of Madeira Cake. Increase the amounts proportionally for larger cakes.
• **Cherry:** Add 175 g (6 oz) glacé cherries, halved.
• **Citrus:** Replace the milk with lemon, orange or lime juice. Add 1 teaspoon of grated lemon, orange or lime rind.
• **Coconut:** Add 50 g (2 oz) desiccated coconut.
• **Nut:** Add 125 g (4 oz) ground almonds, hazelnuts, walnuts or pecan nuts.

Quantity Chart for Madeira Cake

Square tin						
15 cm (6 inch)	18 cm (7 inch)	20 cm (8 inch)	23 cm (9 inch)	25 cm (10 inch)	28 cm (11 inch)	30 cm (12 inch)
Round tin						
18 cm (7 inch)	20 cm (8 inch)	23 cm (9 inch)	25 cm (10 inch)	28 cm (11 inch)	30 cm (12 inch)	33 cm (13 inch)
Plain flour						
250 g (8 oz)	375 g (12 oz)	500 g (1 lb)	550 g (1 lb 2 oz)	675 g (1 lb 6 oz)	750 g (1½ lb)	1 kg (2 lb)
Baking powder						
1 teaspoon	1½ teaspoons	2 teaspoons	2½ teaspoons	3 teaspoons	3½ teaspoons	4 teaspoons
Caster sugar						
175 g (6 oz)	300 g (10 oz)	425 g (14 oz)	500 g (1 lb)	550 g (1 lb 2 oz)	675 g (1 lb 6 oz)	900 g (1 lb 10 oz)
Soft margarine						
175 g (6 oz)	300 g (10 oz)	425 g (14 oz)	500 g (1 lb)	550 g (1 lb 2 oz)	675 g (1 lb 6oz)	900 g (1 lb 10 oz)
Size 3 eggs						
3	5	7	8	10	12	13
Milk						
2 tablespoons	3 tablespoons	3½ tablespoons	4 tablespoons	4½ tablespoons	5 tablespoons	5½ tablespoons
Approx. cooking time						
1¼–1½ hours	1½–1¾ hours	1¾–2 hours	1¾–2 hours	2–2¼ hours	2¼–2½ hours	2½–2¾ hours

Light Fruit Cake

Grease and line a deep cake tin. Stir together the mixed dried fruit, mixed cut peel, stem ginger, almonds, orange rind, orange juice and sherry in a large mixing bowl.

Sift the flour and mixed spice into another bowl. Add the sugar, butter or margarine and eggs. Mix together with a wooden spoon, then beat for about 2–3 minutes until smooth and glossy, or beat for 1 minute in an electric mixer. Gradually add the fruit mixture to the creamed mixture and fold it in, using a spatula, until all the fruit is evenly mixed.

Spoon the mixture into the prepared cake tin and spread it out evenly. Give the tin a few sharp taps to level the mixture and remove any air pockets. Smooth the surface with the back of a metal spoon, making a fairly deep depression in the centre.

Bake in a preheated oven, 140°C (275°F), Gas Mark 1, for the time specified on the chart. Test the cake 15 minutes before the end of the given cooking time. If it is cooked, the cake should feel firm, and a fine skewer inserted into the centre should come out clean.

If the cake is not cooked, return it to the oven and re-test at 15-minute intervals.

Remove from the oven and leave to cool completely in the tin. If desired, use the same amount of alcohol as used in the recipe for the cake (see chart), spooning half the quantity over the top of the cake and wrapping in foil. Store in a cool place for a week. Unwrap the cake and then spoon over another half quantity of alcohol. Re-wrap the cake and store for up to 4 weeks.

Quantity Chart for Light Fruit Cake

Square tin

12 cm (5 inch)	15 cm (6 inch)	18 cm (7 inch)	20 cm (8 inch)	23 cm (9 inch)	25 cm (10 inch)	28 cm (11 inch)	30 cm (12 inch)

Round tin

15 cm (6 inch)	18 cm (7 inch)	20 cm (8 inch)	23 cm (9 inch)	25 cm (10 inch)	28 cm (11 inch)	30 cm (12 inch)	33 cm (13 inch)

Mixed dried fruit

300 g (10 oz)	425 g (14 oz)	500 g (1 lb)	750 g (1½ lb)	1 kg (2 lb)	1.25 kg (2½ lb)	1.5 kg (3 lb)	1.75 kg (3½ lb)

Mixed cut peel

25 g (1 oz)	25 g (1 oz)	40 g (1½ oz)	40 g (1½ oz)	50 g (2 oz)	75 g (3 oz)	125 g (4 oz)	150 g (5 oz)

Stem ginger, chopped

25 g (1 oz)	25 g (1 oz)	50 g (2 oz)	75 g (3 oz)	125 g (4 oz)	150 g (5 oz)	175 g (6 oz)	200 g (7 oz)

Flaked almonds

25 g (1 oz)	25 g (l oz)	50 g (2 oz)	75 g (3 oz)	l25 g (4 oz)	150 g (5 oz)	175 g (6 oz)	200 g (7 oz)

Orange rind, coarsely grated

1 teaspoon	1½ teaspoons	2 teaspoons	3 teaspoons	4 teaspoons	5 teaspoons	6 teaspoons	7 teaspoons

Orange juice

1 tablespoon	1 tablespoon	2 tablespoons	2½ tablespoons	3 tablespoons	3½ tablespoons	4 tablespoons	4½ tablespoons

Sherry

1 tablespoon	1 tablespoon	2 tablespoons	2½ tablespoons	3 tablespoons	3½ tablespoons	4 tablespoons	4½ tablespoons

Plain flour

250 g (8 oz)	300 g (10 oz)	375 g (12 oz)	500 g (1 lb)	625 g (1¼ lb)	750 g (1½ lb)	875 g (1¾ lb)	1 kg (2 lb)

Ground mixed spice

1 teaspoon	1½ teaspoons	2 teaspoons	3 teaspoons	4 teaspoons	5 teaspoons	6 teaspoons	7 teaspoons

Light soft brown sugar

175 g (6 oz)	250 g (8 oz)	300 g (10 oz)	425 g (14 oz)	525 g (1 lb 1 oz)	625 g (1¼ lb)	750 g (1½ lb)	875 g (1¾ lb)

Butter or margarine, softened

175 g (6 oz)	250 g (8 oz)	300 g (10 oz)	425 g (14 oz)	525 g (1 lb 1 oz)	625 g (1¼ lb)	750 g (1½ lb)	875 g (1¾ lb)

Size 3 eggs

3	4	4	5	6	7	8	9

Approx. cooking time

2¼–2½ hours	2½–2¾ hours	2¾–3¼ hours	3¼–3¾ hours	3½–4 hours	4–4½ hours	4½–4¾ hours	4¾–5½ hours

Victoria Sandwich Cake

125 g (4 oz) butter or margarine
125 g (4 oz) caster sugar
2 eggs
125 g (4 oz) self-raising flour, sifted
1 tablespoon hot water

Line and grease two 18 cm (7 inch) sandwich tins. Cream the fat and sugar together until light and fluffy. Beat in the eggs, one at a time, adding a tablespoon of flour with the second egg. Fold in the remaining flour, then the hot water.

Spoon the cake mixture into the prepared tins and then bake in a preheated oven, 180°C (350°F), Gas Mark 4, for 20–25 minutes or until the cakes spring back when pressed lightly with a finger. Turn out onto a wire rack to cool.

Makes one 18 cm (7 inch) round cake

Flavourings
• **Coffee:** Add 1 tablespoon instant coffee powder with the flour.
• **Chocolate:** Add 1 tablespoon sifted cocoa powder with the flour.
• **Citrus:** Add the grated rind of 1 orange or lemon with the fat and sugar.
• **Vanilla:** Add a few drops of vanilla essence to the cake mixture.

Rich Fruit Cake

This recipe makes a very moist rich cake suitable for any celebration cake. It allows the cake to be made in stages, especially if time is short or if you are making more than one cake. The quantities have been worked out so that the depth of each cake is the same. This is important when making several tiers for a wedding cake.

Mix the raisins, sultanas, currants, glacé cherries, mixed peel, flaked almonds, lemon rind and juice, and brandy or sherry in a large mixing bowl. Cover the bowl with clingfilm and then leave for several hours or overnight.

Sift the flour and mixed spice into another bowl. Add the ground almonds, sugar, butter or margarine, treacle and eggs. Mix together with a wooden spoon, and then beat for about 2–3 minutes until smooth and glossy.

Gradually add the mixed fruit to the creamed mixture and fold it in until all the fruit has been evenly blended. Spoon the mixture into the prepared tin and spread it out evenly. Give the tin a few sharp taps to level the mixture and to remove any air pockets. Smooth the surface with the back of a metal spoon, making a slight depression in the centre. Cover with some clingfilm and leave overnight in a cool place, if wished.

Bake the cake in the centre of a preheated oven, 140°C (275°F), Gas Mark 1, for the time specified on the chart. Test the cake to see if it is cooked 30 minutes before the end of the cooking time. If it is cooked, the cake should feel firm and a fine skewer inserted into the centre should come out clean. If the cake is not cooked, retest it at 15-minute intervals. Remove the cake from the oven and allow it to cool in the tin.

Turn out of the tin but don't remove the lining paper as it helps to keep the moisture in. Spoon half of the quantity of alcohol over the top of the cake and wrap it in a double thickness of foil.

Store the cake in a cool, dry place on its base with the top uppermost for a week. Unwrap the cake and spoon over the remaining alcohol. Rewrap the cake and store upside-down, so that the brandy or sherry moistens the top and helps to keep it flat. This cake will store well for up to 3 months.

Quantity Chart for Rich Fruit Cake

Square tin

12 cm (5 inch)	15 cm (6 inch)	18 cm (7 inch)	20 cm (8 inch)	23 cm (9 inch)	25 cm (10 inch)	28 cm (11 inch)	30 cm (12 inch)

Round tin

15 cm (6 inch)	18 cm (7 inch)	20 cm (8 inch)	23 cm (9 inch)	25 cm (10 inch)	28 cm (11 inch)	30 cm (12 inch)	33 cm (13 inch)
Raisins							
200 g (7 oz)	275 g (9 oz)	325 g (11 oz)	400 g (13 oz)	500 g (1 lb)	625 g (1 lb 4 oz)	750 g (1 lb 8 oz)	875 g (1 lb 12 oz)
Sultanas							
125 g (4 oz)	175 g (6 oz)	250 g (8 oz)	300 g (10 oz)	400 g (13 oz)	525 g (1 lb 1 oz)	625 g (1 lb 4 oz)	750 g (1 lb 8 oz)
Currants							
75 g (3 oz)	125 g (4 oz)	175 g (6 oz)	250 g (8 oz)	325 g (11 oz)	425 g (14 oz)	525 g (1 lb 1 oz)	625 g (1 lb 4 oz)
Glacé cherries, halved							
75 g (3 oz)	75 g (3 oz)	150 g (5 oz)	175 g (6 oz)	200 g (7 oz)	250 g (8 oz)	300 g (10 oz)	375 g (12 oz)
Cut mixed peel							
25 g (1 oz)	45 g (1½ oz)	50 g (2 oz)	75 g (3 oz)	125 g (4 oz)	175 g (6 oz)	250 g (8 oz)	300 g (10 oz)
Flaked almonds							
25 g (1 oz)	40 g (1½ oz)	50 g (2 oz)	75 g (3 oz)	125 g (4 oz)	175 g (6 oz)	250 g (8 oz)	300 g (10 oz)
Lemon rind, coarsely grated							
I teaspoon	1½ teaspoons	2 teaspoons	2½ teaspoons	1 tablespoon	1½ tablespoons	1½ tablespoons	2 tablespoons
Lemon juice							
1 tablespoon	1½ tablespoons	2 tablespoons	3½ tablespoons	4 tablespoons	4½ tablespoons	5 tablespoons	6 tablespoons
Brandy or sherry							
1 tablespoon	2 tablespoons	3 tablespoons	4 tablespoons	5 tablespoons	6 tablespoons	7 tablespoons	8 tablespoons
Plain flour							
175 g (6 oz)	200 g (7 oz)	275 g (9 oz)	325 g (11 oz)	425 g (14 oz)	550 g (1 lb 2 oz)	675 g (1lb 6 oz)	800 g (1 lb 10 oz)
Ground mixed spice							
1 teaspoon	1½ teaspoons	2½ teaspoons	1 tablespoon	1¼ tablespoons	1½ tablespoons	2 tablespoons	3½ tablespoons
Ground almonds							
25 g (1 oz)	40 g (1½ oz)	65 g (2½ oz)	125 g (4 oz)	150 g (5 oz)	250 g (8 oz)	300 g (10 oz)	375 g (12 oz)
Dark brown soft sugar							
125 g (4 oz)	150 g (5 oz)	200 g (7 oz)	275 g (9 oz)	375 g (12 oz)	525 g (1 lb 1 oz)	625 g (1 lb 4 oz)	700 g (1 lb 7 oz)
Butter or margarine, softened							
125 g (4 oz)	150 g (5 oz)	200 g (7 oz)	275 g (9 oz)	375 g (12 oz)	525 g (1 lb 1 oz)	625 g (1 lb 4 oz)	700 g (1 lb 7 oz)
Black treacle							
½ teaspoon	1 tablespoon	1½ tablespoons	2 tablespoons	2½ tablespoons	3 tablespoons	3½ tablespoons	4 tablespoons
Eggs							
2	3	4	5	7	8	10	11
Cooking times							
2¼ hours	2¼–2½ hours	2½–3 hours	3¼–3½ hours	3½–3¾ hours	3¾–4 hours	4–4¼ hours	4½–4¾ hours

Basic Techniques

How to marzipan a cake

Unwrap the cake and remove the lining paper. Place the cake on a cake board and roll the top lightly with a rolling pin to flatten slightly. Brush the top of the cake with some apricot glaze.

Lightly dust the work surface with icing sugar. Using two-thirds of the marzipan, knead it into a round. Roll it out to a 5 mm (¼ inch) thickness to match the shape of the top of the cake, allowing a little extra.

1 Invert the cake onto the marzipan. Trim off the excess marzipan to within 1 cm (½ inch) of the cake and push the marzipan level against the side. Turn the cake the right way up and place on a cake board.

2 Brush the sides of the cake with apricot glaze. Roll out the marzipan to 5 mm (¼ inch) thickness and cut out 1 single side piece for a round cake or 4 pieces for a square cake. Gently unroll the side strip and fit to the sides of the cake.

3 Use a palette knife to smooth the joins. Leave the cake in a warm, dry place for at least 24 hours to allow it to dry thoroughly before icing it.

To ice a round cake board

Place the cake on its board on a turntable and spread a thin layer of icing over the cake board. Neaten the edge with a palette knife.

Hold the side scraper close to the board and then turn the cake and turntable one revolution, drawing the edge of the scraper towards you to smooth the icing. Neaten the edge with a palette knife and then leave to dry. Repeat with a second layer of icing.

To ice a square cake board

Follow the instructions for icing a round board, but ice the opposite edges at a time. Smooth with a side scraper and neaten the edges; leave to dry. Repeat to ice the remaining edges and leave to dry. Repeat with a second layer of icing.

Icing run-outs

These are one of the most useful forms of cake decoration. They can be made in any shape or form by simply tracing over a chosen design or pattern. Once made, they can be kept successfully between layers of waxed paper in a box stored in a dry place. This means a quantity of run-outs can be made in advance to be attached to the cake at a later date.

Run-outs are made from royal icing. Because they are very fragile, it is wise to choose a solid shape for your first attempts. Make more than the design requires to allow for breakages. Accuracy, not speed, is important when making run-outs, so always allow plenty of time. The consistency and texture of the royal icing used for run-outs must be right or they will be difficult to make and hard to handle. Use double-strength dried egg albumen or egg whites, with no additives such as glycerine or lemon juice. The icing should be light and glossy, not heavy and dull. When the spoon is lifted, a sharp peak should form which will stay pointed at the tip. This is the consistency required for piping the outline of the run-outs.

The icing to fill in the run-out must be soft enough to flow with the help of a paint brush, just holding its shape until tapped, then becoming smooth. Leave the icing to stand overnight if possible, covered with damp muslin, allowing any air bubbles to come to the surface. Stir until smooth before using.

1 Draw or trace the chosen design several times on a piece of paper and secure to a flat surface with sticky tape or beads of icing. Cover with waxed paper and fix in place with beads of icing. Using a No. 1 plain writing nozzle, pipe around the outline with one continuous thread of icing.

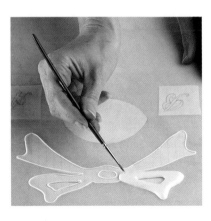

3 Using a fine paint brush or a cocktail stick, spread the icing very gently to ensure that the area is completely covered and that the icing is smooth. Gently tap the board so that any air bubbles rise to the surface; burst them with a pin.

2 Snip the pointed end of a piping bag filled with soft icing and fill in the run-out. Start by piping around the inside edge to keep the outline soft, otherwise it may break, and then work towards the centre, filling the shape so that the icing looks rounded, not flat, because the icing shrinks as it sets.

4 Leave the run-outs in a warm, dry place overnight until they have set quite hard. The more quickly they dry, the glossier the run-outs will be. If wished, you can pipe a bead design onto the completely dried run-outs. Carefully peel off the waxed paper and store the run-outs in a box between layers of new waxed paper.

Piping

To practise piping, use a greaseproof paper piping bag fitted with a straight-sided metal nozzle as this gives a clean, sharp icing pattern.

Half-fill the bag with icing; do not be tempted to fill it to the top as it will be much harder to squeeze the icing out of the nozzle.

Hold the piping bag comfortably with the nozzle through the first two fingers and thumb, like holding a pencil, applying the pressure at the top of the bag. The wrists and arms should be relaxed, just ready to guide the nozzle.

1 To make a piping bag, cut out a 38 x 25 cm (15 x 10 inch) rectangle of greaseproof paper and fold in half diagonally to form 2 triangles, each with a blunt end. Cut along the fold with a knife.

2 Use one of the greaseproof paper triangles and fold the blunt end over to the centre to form a sharp cone. Hold in position and then fold the sharp end of the triangle over the cone shape.

3 Align all the points at the back of the cone, ensuring that the point of the cone is sharp. Turn the points inside the top edge of the cone and crease firmly. Secure the cone with sticky tape, if desired.

4 With some sharp scissors, cut off the tip of the cone and insert a piping nozzle, according to the sort of piping you wish to do.

5 Do not fill the piping bag more than half full with icing. Fold down the top of the bag and then gently squeeze the icing down to the end of the nozzle.

right: 1 Swirls; 2 Stars; 3 Reverse scrolls; 4 Shell edging; 5 Straight lines; 6 Basket weave piping; 7 Leaves or petal shapes piped from a greaseproof paper piping bag with the end snipped into an inverted 'V'.

Piping with a star nozzle

Use a simple star icing nozzle and fit it into a greaseproof paper piping bag to pipe swirls, scrolls and shells.

• **Swirls:** Half-fill the greaseproof paper piping bag, fold down the top and squeeze the icing to the end of the nozzle. Place the icing nozzle just on to the surface of the cake and pipe a swirl of icing in a circular movement. Stop pressing the bag and pull up sharply to break the icing. Repeat to pipe swirls around the top edge and base of the cake, if desired.

• **Stars:** Hold the bag straight above the surface of the cake. Press the icing out to form a star on the edge of the cake, then pull off to break the icing; repeat to make a neat border.

• **Scrolls:** Hold the piping bag at an angle so that the piping nozzle is almost on its side in front of you. Pipe some icing on to the top edge of the cake to secure the scroll. Pipe outwards in a circular movement and return the piping nozzle to the edge of the cake. Stop pressing the bag and break off the icing. Repeat again but pipe the icing away from the cake in a circular movement, then return the nozzle just to the edge. This is piping scrolls inwards and outwards. For a different design, pipe the scrolls in one direction only.

• **Shells:** Hold the piping bag at an angle to the cake so that the piping nozzle is almost on its side in front of you. Press out some icing and secure to the surface of the cake, pressing gently; move the nozzle forwards, then move it slowly up, over and down almost like a rocking movement. Stop pressing and break off the icing by pulling the nozzle towards you. Repeat piping the icing on to the end of the first shell to make a shell edging.

• **Lines:** Fit the piping bag with a plain writing nozzle and fill it with icing. Pipe a thread of icing, securing the end to the surface of the cake. Continue to pipe the icing just above the surface of the cake, allowing the thread to fall in a straight or curved line. Stop pressing and break off the icing.

• **Basket weave pattern:** Fit a greaseproof paper piping bag with a ribbon nozzle. Pipe a vertical line from the top of the cake to the bottom. Pipe 2 cm (¾ inch) lines across the vertical line at 1.5 cm (½ inch) intervals. Pipe another vertical line of icing on the edge of the horizontal lines, then pipe short lines of icing in between the spaces across the vertical line to form a basket weave. Repeat in the same way all around the cake.

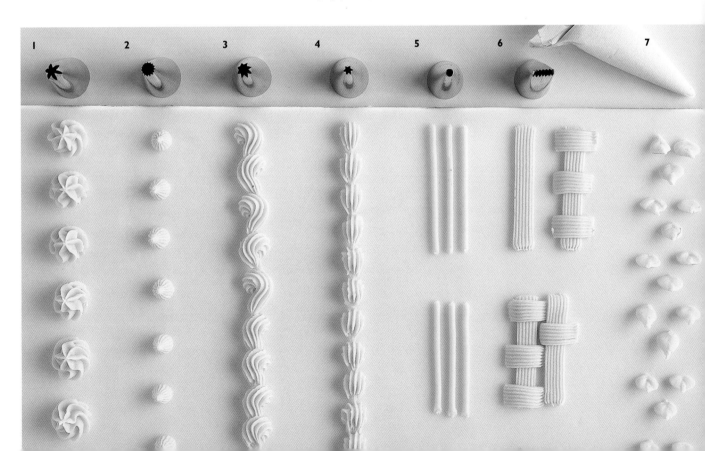

7

Feather Icing

Colour one-third of the recipe quantity of glacé icing (see page 73) a pale colour with food colouring. Place in a greaseproof paper piping bag and snip off the point.

Quickly spread the cake surface evenly with white glacé icing and immediately pipe lines or dots of coloured icing, equally spaced apart, on the top.

Draw a cocktail stick or a fine skewer lightly across the lines or dots of icing in alternate directions to form a feather pattern.

To vary the pattern, pipe some concentric circles of coloured icing over the top of the cake and draw a cocktail stick or skewer from the centre to the edge in alternate directions to make a cobweb design.

Sugar-frosted Flowers

Always choose fresh, simple, small flowers, such as violets, primroses, miniature daffodils, freesias and fuchsias or rose petals.

1 egg white, lightly beaten
caster sugar

Dry the flowers with kitchen paper, leaving a small stem if possible. Brush both sides of the flowers with some beaten egg white.

Spoon the sugar over the flowers to coat them evenly, and shake carefully to remove any excess. Place on a wire rack covered with kitchen paper, and leave in a warm place until dry.

Modelling roses: flowers and leaves

Modelling paste is firm enough to roll out very thinly, dries quickly and keeps its shape. It is ideal for modelling delicate roses.

1 rounded teaspoon gelatine
1 rounded teaspoon white fat
5 teaspoons cold water
250 g (8 oz) icing sugar

Place the gelatine, fat and water in a small saucepan. Heat gently until the gelatine has dissolved and the liquid is clear. Gradually stir in the icing sugar until the mixture forms a firm ball.

Turn out and knead in the remaining icing sugar – you may need a little more – until the paste is firm but pliable. Always keep the paste covered in a polythene bag or clingfilm to prevent drying.

Modelling rose buds: Very lightly grease the work surface, your hands and the rolling pin with white fat. Take a small piece of modelling paste and form into a cone shape. Roll out a small ball of paste into a strip and wind the strip around the top of the cone, covering the tip completely so that it looks like the tightly curled centre of a rose.

Modelling roses: Roll out small balls of paste into petal shapes, flattening the

edges between your finger and thumb. Brush the base of each petal very lightly with egg white and press in turn onto the rose bud (see above), overlapping the petals until the rose is the required size. It will look more realistic if the edge of each petal is rolled back slightly.

Modelling rose leaves: Pick and clean a rose leaf from the garden and very lightly grease the underside of the leaf. Press green-coloured paste onto the underside of the leaf and carefully break the paste away from the edges of the leaf to create a jagged effect. Carefully pull the paste away from the leaf and the veins will appear on the paste. Leave to dry, curved over crumpled kitchen paper. If there are no real rose leaves available, simply cut out oval leaf shapes and mark the veins with the back of a knife, or use a flower cutter.

Marzipan or modelling paste leaves: Colour a little marzipan or modelling paste with green and possibly a touch of blue liquid food colouring to give a good leaf colour. Knead until evenly coloured. If it becomes sticky, knead in a little sifted icing sugar. Roll out thinly and cut out rose leaf shapes with a sharp knife. If you can't do this freehand, cut out a leaf shape from card and use this as a guide. Using a sharp knife, mark a vein and side veins on the leaf and put to dry on nonstick baking paper. If curved leaves are preferred, lay them over a wooden spoon handle to dry completely.

Marzipan or modelling paste roses: Use 250 g (8 oz) marzipan or modelling

paste to make approximately 30 roses. Colour the marzipan or moulding paste a deep ruby red (or any other colour you require) by kneading in liquid food colourings. Roll out some of the icing very thinly and then cut into circles of 1–2 cm (½–¾ inch) diameter. Taking one circle at a time, hold at one side and, with the fingers of the other hand, carefully press out the circle until very thin and almost transparent. If necessary, dip your fingers in cornflour to prevent sticking. Roll the first one up for the centre and wrap a second petal around it fairly tightly at the base, but leaving it looser at the top to show the centre. This makes a rose bud. Continue to make 2 more petals in the same way, adding a dab of water if necessary to make it stick. Fold the outer petals outwards slightly. This will make a medium-sized rose. Continue adding 2 or 3 more petals, each a fraction larger than the last, to give a large rose. The roses can be made up to 1 month before required.

Marzipan holly leaves and berries: Make a dark green marzipan by moulding green, blue and a touch of brown food colouring into 75 g (3 oz) marzipan. Roll out thinly and cut into rectangles about 4 cm (1½ inches) long and 2 cm (¾ inch) wide. Using a tiny round petit four cutter or the base of a piping nozzle, make the leaves by taking cuts out of the edges of the marzipan rectangles. Mark a vein down the centre with a sharp knife and leave to dry on greased greaseproof or nonstick baking paper or, for curved leaves, lay over the greased handle of a wooden spoon.

Alternatively, use a holly leaf cutter.

For the berries, tint a small piece of marzipan a deep red and shape into tiny balls, rolling them between the palms of the hand. Leave to dry in a warm place for at least 24 hours to prevent their colour seeping into the white icing.

Carnations: Tint some decoration or gelatine icing with pink and lilac food colourings (or leave white). Roll and cut out 5 cm (2 inch) circles and roll the edges with a cocktail stick. Brush the centres with a little egg white and fold in half. Repeat and fold in half again. Leave to dry overnight on crumpled cling film before using.

White frilled flowers: Roll out some decoration icing and cut out some 1 cm (½ inch) circles with a fluted cutter. Use a cocktail stick to flute the edges and dry overnight on a tray lined with some greaseproof paper.

Primroses: Shape a small cone of yellow marzipan over the end of a paint brush. Make 5 dents around the top edge with a cocktail stick. Cut between the dents to form 5 petals. Flatten them between your fingers and then open them out, curving the corners.

Daffodils: Model 6 yellow petal shapes per flower, lightly making a line down the centre of each. Take a small ball of yellow decoration icing and push in a plain nozzle to make a wide hole. Roll the edge with a cocktail stick to flute the trumpet. Stand, flute-side down, and overlap the petals around the base, securing with egg white. Dry overnight.

Chocolate Leaves

Choose real leaves which are small and have well-defined veins. Glossy leaves, such as those from roses, geraniums or camellias, are good, but soft leaves, such as mint, will wilt with the warmth of the chocolate.

Use 125 g (4 oz) white, plain dark or milk chocolate, melted. Try to leave a small stem on each leaf and wash and dry thoroughly before using to make chocolate leaves. You will need a clean, fine paint brush and some nonstick baking paper.

1 Using a clean, fine paint brush, thickly coat the underside of each washed and dried leaf with melted chocolate, taking care not to paint over the edge of the leaf.

2 Place the painted leaves on a sheet of nonstick baking paper and leave to dry, chocolate side up, in a cool place. Carefully peel the leaves away from the set chocolate.

3 The finished chocolate leaves, ready to use for decorating cakes and gâteaux, look very attractive and delicate. Treat them with care to prevent breakages.

Chocolate Curls

Pour 125 g (4 oz) plain, milk or white chocolate, melted, on to a rigid surface, such as marble, wood or plastic laminate. Spread evenly backwards and forwards with a palette knife until it begins to set.

When the chocolate is set but not hard, use a sharp knife held at an angle of about 45° to the chocolate. Draw the knife across the surface to shave off thin layers of chocolate which form into curls. To make large curls – caraque – draw the knife down the whole length of the chocolate.

Make chocolate shavings in the same way, but let the chocolate set a little harder, then draw the knife only halfway across the surface to make half curls.

Chocolate run-outs

Choose any simple shape for your decorations, such as animals, birds, hearts, flowers, bells, horseshoes, numerals and letters, or use a shaped cutter.

Draw round the cutter or draw or trace the chosen shape on a piece of paper, making more than you will finally need to allow for breakages. Place a sheet of nonstick baking paper over the top and stick down the edges.

Using a greaseproof paper piping bag filled with melted chocolate, snip off the point and pipe a thread of chocolate around the edge of the design.

Fill in the outline with melted chocolate, using enough to give a rounded finish. Leave to set. Pipe in any details if necessary, then let it set hard.

Carefully peel off the baking paper and use the run-out decorations as desired.

Chocolate Cut-out Pieces

Use 125 g (4 oz) milk, plain dark or white chocolate, melted. Pour it on to a sheet of nonstick baking paper and then spread it out as evenly as possible with a palette knife. Pick up the corners of the paper and let

them drop a few times to level the chocolate and also to remove any air bubbles.

When the chocolate can be touched without sticking to the fingers and it is still pliable, place another piece of baking paper on top. Turn the whole sheet of chocolate over, peel off the backing paper, and then turn the chocolate over again.

1 Press the cutter down firmly onto the chocolate, then lift it up and carefully remove the shape.

2 Cut the chocolate rounds into triangles or semi-circles and ovals, using a smaller cutter.

3 Measure and make the size of squares required, using a sharp knife and a straight edge or ruler.

4 Use a sharp knife to cut along the marked lines and remove the shapes. Cut diagonally for triangles.

Templates

To make your own templates, you can trace simple designs from Christmas or birthday cards or children's books. Alternatively, you can draw your own designs onto tracing paper or trace one of the templates drawn here for decorating some of the special and novelty cakes featured in this book.

Cut out the template of your choice and place it on top of the cake. Pipe around the outline and then remove the template and flood in with softened icing. Or you can trace the template onto fondant, decoration or gelatine icing (white or coloured) and then cut out the desired shape.

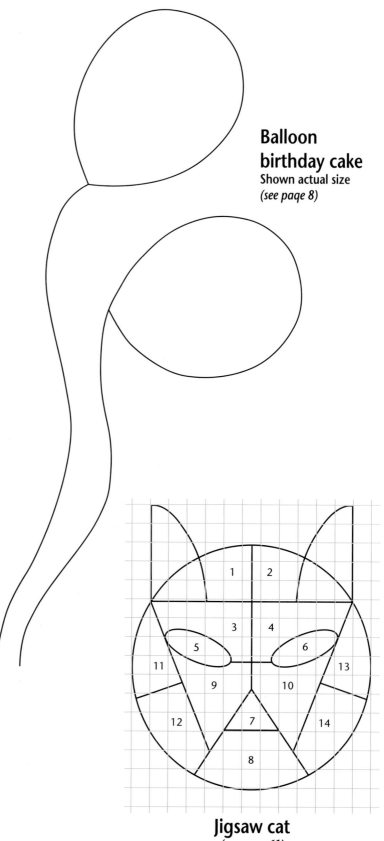

Balloon birthday cake
Shown actual size
(see page 8)

Jigsaw cat
(see page 61)

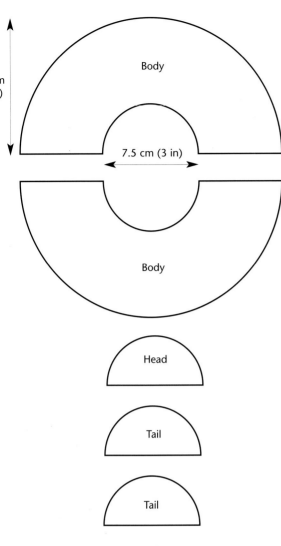

cm
in)

Body

7.5 cm (3 in)

Body

Head

Tail

Tail

Dennis dinosaur
(see page 65)

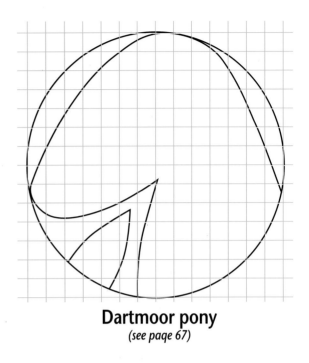

Dartmoor pony
(see page 67)

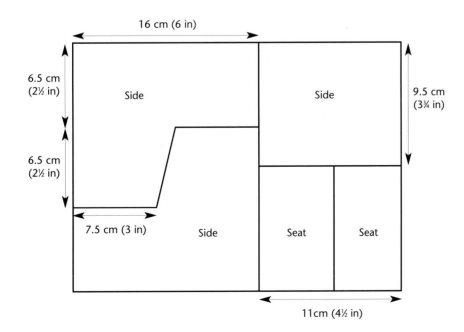

16 cm (6 in)

6.5 cm
(2½ in)

Side

Side

9.5 cm
(3¾ in)

6.5 cm
(2½ in)

7.5 cm (3 in)

Side

Seat

Seat

11cm (4½ in)

Happily retired *(see page 56)*

Index